PRAISE FOR
GOD WITHOUT GUILT

"God Without Guilt is a word in season for those in the body of Christ who have been wounded by the vicious spirit of religion and for those discouraged by the vast void of truth from a vacuous pulpit. It is also a word in season for the ones wandering outside of the body of Christ, those who have never heard the authentic voice of a living God who loves them, and desires to draw them near to Him.

Randolph Perry-Smith's voice is consistent, clear and convincing to anyone who would suffer under the condemnation of religion. His invitation in *God Without Guilt* is for all of us to know the true God, and experience His unfailing love, maybe for the first time in our lives."

— ***Sandra Leslie White,*** missionary, minister and messenger, Hosea International Ministries, and author of *My God, My Man*

"If you want to do a deep dive into what the Bible teaches on grace, this is a book for you."

— ***Dr. Bob Beltz,*** pastor, speaker, film producer, author of *Somewhere Fast: Becoming a Man of Prayer* and *The Spirit*

"Randolph is a voice and not an echo."

— ***Pastor Henry L. Boyens,*** president of Arising Light International

GOD
WITHOUT
GUILT

GOD
WITHOUT
GUILT

REVEALING THE
LOST TREASURE
OF GOD'S LOVE

RANDOLPH T. PERRY-SMITH

ILLUMIFY
MEDIA.COM

God Without Guilt

Copyright © 2025 by Randolph Perry-Smith

The views and opinions expressed in this book are those of the author and do not necessarily reflect the official policy or position of Illumify Media Global.

Published by
Illumify Media Global
www.IllumifyMedia.com
"Let's bring your book to life!"

Library of Congress Control Number: 2025918202

Paperback ISBN: 978-1-964251-84-4

Typeset by Art Innovations (http://artinnovations.in/)
Cover design by Debbie Lewis

Printed in the United States of America

To my grandmother Agnes,
who showed us the love of God.

CONTENTS

FOREWORD

By Dan Hudick

I met Randy when I was in my late twenties or early thirties. He was sharing a house with my rock-climbing partner at the time. Randy was running his own paving business, and I was running an earthmoving business with my brother. Because we had similar businesses, we found commonality quickly. We also shared some crazy inclinations for our distractions. Randy was into extreme skiing, and I thought he was crazy. I was into rock climbing, so he thought I was crazy.

I had spent a great deal of time thinking about God. Like so many people, especially young people, my views on God were mixed. I felt deep down that we were created by a higher power and hadn't evolved from a one-celled, blue-green algae. But I couldn't accept that this "God," who supposedly loved me so much that He sacrificed Himself on the cross for me, would at the same time demand my constant obedience, and in keeping with this, would expect my constant confession and repentance to receive forgiveness. All of this while under the threat of burning in hell if I didn't do these things.

How is that love?

I figured I was a pretty good guy. I did what my father trained me to do: do the right thing, be an honest person, treat people as I wanted to be treated. But if by not doing the things that were required by God, I was to be condemned to hell, how was I to love Him? How do you love someone who judges so harshly?

How is that love?

It wasn't until I saw God's love in action through Randy that I reconsidered my position. Those who start their own businesses often suffer huge disappointment. On that road are long periods of disillusionment. I went through a very rough patch, and I knew Randy had gone through one as well. But he seemed to have weathered it better than I had. I asked him how he maintained his state of happiness as he went through hard times. He said something like, "I love the Lord, and I'm walking with Him."

What?

Randy was a strong guy. Why did he need God to find his happiness? I wanted to know what he knew, so I began a conversation with him. He told me to read the Old Testament book of Ecclesiastes before we talked about God and Jesus. That was the beginning of my quest to know the Lord.

When the disciples asked Jesus how to pray, He gave them a perfect prayer. It starts with "Our Father," not our judge or our almighty forgiving one. I think He wants from us what any father wants from his children: relationship. God loves His children and wants the best for them. He wants us to come to Him with our troubles, our anger, or any state of mind we may be in at the moment. God wants us to share our lives with Him.

Randy helped me understand and accept that God meets me right where I am. It is a gift, not a demand. It is my choice. And whether I am willing or unwilling to accept His invitation, He will never give up on me. He will never give up on you either.

I hope this book—which is written to convey the freedom and joy that comes from having a relationship with God—can be understood in the way my dear friend Randy desired to impart this to you. It became a constant thorn in his side as I nagged at him to commit this to writing. I am so grateful that he finally finished it, because the truth within its pages have helped me know and love the one true God and to enjoy the life that He has given me to live.

ACKNOWLEDGMENTS

*F*irst, I have to thank the Father as our one true God. I thank Him for Jesus, His Son, who reconciled us to the Father, and for the Holy Spirt who raised Christ from death to life and who gives us life, direction, and understanding in the Father. I believe the apostle Paul said it best in the opening of the book of Philippians:

> And it is my prayer that your love may abound more and more, with knowledge and all discernment, so that you may approve what is excellent, and so be pure and blameless for the day of Christ, filled with the fruit of righteousness that comes through Jesus Christ, to the glory and praise of God. (Philippians 1:9–11 ESV)

That is the reason I wrote this book. My prayer is that your love would abound and that you would grow with knowledge and discernment of Christ and the Bible. I pray that you may know that your righteousness comes through the finished work of Jesus on the cross. It is not through your good works or behavior.

Starting with the order of my understanding, I thank my first pastor, Dale Schlafer, for teaching me never to trust the word of a pastor alone but to research Scripture myself. This statement became anchored in my mind and was the catalyst of my always challenging what is taught from the pulpit.

Dr. Bob Beltz, who has always given me food for thought in his Bible teaching, modeled to me that it helps to utilize humor while learning, and he encouraged me to write this book.

Three radio pastors taught me the freedom I have in Christ Jesus: Aaron Budjen with Living God Ministries, Colin Cook with How It Happens, and Bob George with People to People.

Dr. J. Vernon McGee, in Thru the Bible, reinforced the importance of understanding the etymology of Greek and Hebrew words. His encouragement to look up the origins of words is responsible for my enhanced understanding of the Bible.

Bible Study Fellowship propelled my interest to study the Bible with depth. The homework assignments and excellent questions brought accountability in my quest to understand God's Word. The interaction in small groups showed me the sincerity of men who fight the good fight to live in the Spirit. I sincerely believe Bible

Study Fellowship is the way of a true Church. I disagreed with many of the legalistic viewpoints, but the fellowship in the groups was loving. I saw no greater example of the presence of God among us. I spent fourteen years with these brothers, and I look forward to continued attendance.

Two great online sources assisted in my understanding of the Greek and Hebrew words in the Bible. I believe that both Bible Hub and the Blue Letter Bible will enrich your study of God's Word. I also encourage everyone to own a Bible dictionary to quick reference names, places, and history.

A big acknowledgment goes to my best friend Dan Hudick. His encouragement and support helped make this book possible.

Thanks to Lori Janke, who took years of my notes and writings and arranged them to bring order to my thoughts. The process she went through unlocked this book.

So much of the Bible I did not understand. I would read it and say to myself, *This does not make sense.* But God wants us to understand His Word and be able to make sense of it. I prayed for His insight and wisdom and for Him to help me make sense of His Word. Many of my prayers are answered in the following pages. There is always more to learn from the Bible, but I hope this adds to your knowledge and provokes thought. The hardest thing I have ever had to learn is to rest in the finished work of Jesus. Blessings as you read this work.

INTRODUCTION

IT IS NOT ABOUT
SIN AND GUILT

I believe the biggest mistake in our understanding of the gospel and its presentation to believers and unbelievers is the emphasis on sin and guilt. Many have turned away from God because of the condemnation in the message. Guilt does not bring anyone into closer relationship. In fact, it makes us hide from God.

Beginning with the Fall and the separation of man from God (Genesis 1–3), sin has been with human beings. It is our nature and is as common as breathing. We sin knowingly and unknowingly. If guilt from sin is the main emphasis for knowing God, we will be driven from Him. If you have ever loaned money to someone who was unable to repay, you probably found that their guilt would cause them to avoid you.

This emphasis on sin makes us constantly believe we are in debt to God for our shortcomings. But that is not the reason Jesus suffered and died. Paul states, "Or do you show contempt for the riches of his kindness, forbearance and patience, not realizing that God's kindness is intended to lead you to repentance?"(Romans 2:4). We can follow this with a reminder from John:

> For God so loved the world he gave his one and only Son, that whoever believes in him shall not perish but have eternal life. For God did not send his Son into the world to condemn the world, but to save the world through him. Whoever believes in him is not condemned, but whoever does not believe stands condemned already because they have not believed in the name of God's one and only Son. (John 3:16–18)

Jesus did not come to condemn us but to save us and give us life through faith in Him. God's love and His desire for relationship with us is the main theme of the Bible—from beginning to end. To have a relationship with us is the reason He sent His Son. Faith and life in God are the themes of the Bible—not the sin and guilt of our ways. Faith in Jesus and trusting Him is what God wants from us. We are birthed into this limited life without the Spirit of God. Emptiness exists, and without His Spirit we are dead. Christ came to give us eternal life and to fill us with His Spirit, which is not limited but eternal.

Grace is undeserved merit. Nothing we can do will bring us to God except faith in Him. The gift of grace by which you are saved is the theme of the New Testament. It is repeated over and over. It is a gift to take the sting from sin, guilt, and death. I hear Christians tell unbelievers that God loves them just as they are, but first they must confess they are a rotten, sinful person. This is not the message of grace. I came to Christ because I wanted to know God and understand His thoughts and message. "Everyone who believes that Jesus is the Christ has been born of God, and everyone who loves the Father loves whoever has been born of him" (1 John 5:1 ESV).

If you become a believer but constantly ask for forgiveness of your sin, it means that you believe that God is holding something against you that needs forgiveness. God holds nothing against us save one thing: that we believe Jesus is God and that He came in the flesh to gather us to Himself in love, grace, and unconditional forgiveness of sin. Once again, Christ took away the sin of the whole world for both the believer and unbeliever. "He is the propitiation for our sins, and not for ours only but also for the sins of the whole world" (1 John 2:2 ESV).

When I am sharing Jesus with unbelievers, I am often confronted with their serious concern of whether or not they can change and live like a Christian. Why has the message become one of performance rather than having a relationship with God? The first person to whom Jesus revealed Himself as the Christ was the woman at the well. She was a person who had been married five times and was presently living with a man out of wedlock. Did Jesus shame her or make her feel guilty? No. In response to His acceptance, love, and supernatural knowledge of her situation, she left Him to spread the news of His great message all over town. "But to all who believed him and accepted him, he gave the right to become children of God" (John 1:12 NLT).

Sin confessed is forgiven already by the act of Christ, not because you asked for it. If asking God for forgiveness of sin is what forgives us, why did Christ die on the cross, once and for all? The argument is unless a Christian confesses and asks for forgiveness and repents, Christ somehow does not accept us. That is dangerous thinking. What happened to the unconditional acceptance of love and forgiveness in Christ? Whether or not we believe in Him, nothing stands between us and Christ. He loves us the way we are.

As stated previously, guilt will drive you from Him, while love and acceptance will lead you to Him. Confessing your belief in Him is your act of love and acceptance, and He returns it in kind. We are not condemned or judged. God responds in unconditional love.

The voice I hope to convey as I write is love. I want to come against the horrible picture that man has painted of God and Christianity. I believe that God has been mischaracterized, and we have misjudged what He wants from us. Because of this misunderstanding, most believers have created a works-based faith that draws them further from the peace God desires. They create a belief system that leads them further away from the relationship they desire.

When most Christians are trying to lead someone to Christ, they tell of their own great sins and sin nature. They stress that people need forgiveness from God. I say to you that God forgave you long ago with Jesus on the cross. You had nothing to do with it, and you did not have to ask Him. Let nothing stop you in your belief in Him. He did it all to reconcile you to Him in love.

When Jesus was on the cross, two men hung with Him. One of them, a thief, accepted Jesus as King, the One who has authority. He acknowledged Jesus as God: "Jesus, remember me when you come into your kingdom" (Luke 23:42). He recognized Him as the King with a kingdom!

The kingdom is at hand. The crux of this book is about the love of God with no condemnation. How and why has this message become distorted? I hope that in the following chapters, your love for Jesus grows. The idea that the approval and favor of God are linked to our good behavior is part of what was passed down to us by Adam and Eve. "Adam and Eve chose to live in accordance with the knowledge of good and evil instead of with a dependent personal relationship with their God."[1]

What we feel is enforced by those around us and our environment. We see example after example that good behavior gets rewarded while bad behavior results in rejection, anger, or shame. Religion tells us this message. We are told that to be accepted by God and His Church, we must believe and behave before we can belong.

SIN AND GUILT

My own struggle with this issue lasted twenty years. I wrestled with God over the issues of sin and guilt. I constantly asked God, "How am I going to change to become a follower of Christ?" I would knowingly sin and not include God in my thoughts. God could come everywhere with me—except in my sin. I was playing a spiritual game of hide-and-seek. *I will include God in my life*, I thought, *but I will park Him when I plan on sinning.*

I began to wonder if I had let God down. I wanted to please Him, but I rarely experienced victory over sin. The apostle Paul wrote that he was the worst among sinners (1 Timothy 1:15). In many ways he was. He persecuted the early Christian Church and delighted in the death of Christians. King David was a murder, adulterer, and manipulator, and yet God called him a man after His own heart (1 Samuel 13:14). How would King David or Paul fit into this modern age of Christianity? Better yet, would any church want them in their congregation?

I write this to all secret or blatant sinners who feel condemned in their behavior and have not drawn near to God. I write this to you to let you know it is safe to draw close to your God. I want you to know the loving heart of the One who awaits you. The Bible is a love letter from God to us, and I hope to show you how.

We have a God who loves us no matter what. He is a God who is in pursuit of relationship with us regardless of our circumstances. This is the God I know, and He is Jesus Christ, the Son of God in the Father and the Holy Spirit, full of grace and truth. He is the true God of the Bible.

The last twenty years of my life, I have tried to deconstruct for others the false teachings to which I had fallen prey. Those teachings drove me further from God instead of drawing me closer to Him. I thought the Church existed to encourage growth in my knowledge of God. I have since discovered differently, and I encourage you to draw near to God—not to a church, a school of theology, or a specific pastor. Draw near to God. He loves you as His creation in His image. I would never draw close to a God that would not want me based on how I behaved.

ETYMOLOGY

One of the first things to know when attempting to understand the Bible is that words matter. The etymology of words is very important. This was affirmed to me years ago in a sermon I heard by Dr. James Vernon McGee. A great example of this is the word *enthusiasm*, defined often as excitement. The etymology of the word comes from the Greek word *en*, meaning "with,"[2] and *theos*, meaning "God."[3] The background of this word reveals a much deeper understanding of being with God or having God within us. To be with God or to have Him within is truly exciting, and it is understandable how the meaning has morphed over time.

If we are defining the word *cross*, for example, we would use the meaning of the structure of the cross. The definition would aim to provide a clear and concise explanation of what a cross is, helping the reader to understand the meaning and characteristics of the cross and crucifixion. The focal point of the definition is to accurately and adequately describe its essence, properties, or attributes in a way that clarifies its meaning.

The etymology of the Greek word *stauros*,[4] which also means "cross," finds its origin in the word *histemi*.[5] In this way, the word *cross* comes from the word *stand* or *to take a stand*. Jesus said, "If anyone would come after me, let him deny himself, and take up his cross" (Mathew 16:24 ESV). He meant that those coming after Him would take their stand *for* Him and *in* Him. The most meaningful part of this understanding is the way in which Jesus takes a stand for all mankind, on a stand, the cross, making Himself a public spectacle.

Both Luke and Mark talk about how difficult it is for a rich person to enter the kingdom of God, stating that it is easier for a camel to pass through the eye of a needle (Mark 10:25 and Luke 18:25). Many misunderstand this metaphor made by Jesus. The key that unlocks this is the word *needle*. The etymology of the Greek word *raphis* is *rapizo*, which means "to smite with a rod or a staff."[6]

The interpretation should incorporate this definition, and when that definition is applied, the verse becomes apparent. It is easier for a camel to respond or move (pass) to the sight (eye) of a whip or a rod than for a rich person to enter the kingdom of God. It means a rich person has a hard time identifying who they are in light of authority. Money and wealth can become an idol before the Lord, and this verse serves as a warning for us to trust God and not the riches of the world.

That is my intention—to take Scripture verses that have been understood one way without the correct definitions and shed a different light. My purpose is not to argue with theologians but rather to bring insight as I offer my views. In doing so, perhaps I get to expand the thinking of biblical scholars and laymen.

The only absolute in my understanding of the Bible is that God loves us. Recently I was told by a theologian in my church that doctrine is not based on the metaphors and parables of the Bible. "Are you kidding?" I responded. "The whole book is a metaphor of God's love." I was making the point we do not have to confess how rotten and sinful we are when we come to God.

The greatest example of this is the prodigal son (Luke 15:11–24). The son departs from the father, takes the father's inheritance, and chooses to live a decadent life apart from the father. After the son squanders his inheritance, he returns to the father. The father does not ask the son to confess the error of his ways. Rather, the father sees from a distance the son returning to him. The father starts the celebration before the son arrives and does not require him to confess his mistakes. Again, did Paul, the author of two-thirds of the New Testament, confess his sins and persecution of Christ as he encountered him on the road to Damascus (Acts 9:1–9)? This is the God I know and love, Jesus rejoicing in us turning to Him in faith regardless of what we have done.

I hope to encourage and challenge you to understand the love of God in a greater way. These pages are expressions of the Bible that were given to me by the leading of the Holy Spirit. My purpose is to share them with you to create a greater understanding of His Word.

1

MY STORY OF FAITH

*M*y story of faith began when I was six years old. My siblings and I were instructed to attend a Baptist church. We would walk to church Sunday morning, and I would be placed in the children's group. It was there I learned that if I was baptized, all my sins and bad behavior would be forgiven by God. One evening before bed, I remember thinking I would not be baptized until I was an old man and ready to die. Then I could go before God squeaky clean.

My parents divorced when I was two years old; my mother abandoned me. Instead of growing up with love and security, I grew up with fear, uncertainty, shame, and rage. I was the last child born to my parents. My sister, Christine, who was their third child, did not survive leukemia. She died before I was born. I honestly believe this is why my parents divorced.

There is a high rate of divorce among parents who have lost a child.[1] I believe the reason is the grief. Neither can comfort the other because they both are grieving. Because of their loss of a child and their subsequent divorce, I was abandoned by both of them. Even though my dad had custody of us, he became a workaholic to avoid the pain. My mother remarried, had two more children, and paid little attention to those of us in her former family. We spent some time with her on weekends; however, she never really was emotionally available. I felt like my dad was the same way.

As a result of this, my German grandmother raised me. She was a woman with the love of God in her. Without her, I would have self-destructed. Grandmother Agnes gave us her heart and was very compassionate. I was not punished when I did wrong; instead, I received a look and the words, "You are better than that." Those words would slay me, and still do to this day.

Abandoned children are left feeling rejected, inadequate, or damaged, or feeling as if they need to hide themselves away from others. They feel as if their world is spinning out of control. The worst of my feelings came from my mother abandoning me. I experienced unworthiness because of not having bonded with her. I did not blame her for abandoning me. I couldn't. She was my mother. Instead, I blamed myself. I thought that surely there must be something wrong with me. Whatever I did in my life, it was never enough to gain love and respect from my mother. No matter what, I was never good enough. I needed to control and understand my environment in order to feel safe.

Until her death, my mother continued to reinforce this. Five years before she died, I began calling her once a week in the hopes that we could heal this chasm between us. It didn't work. And then, shortly before she died, I told her how I was endeavoring to write a book. Instead of any encouragement or kind words, she simply shared how her other son, my half-brother, was a talented writer. She never once asked about my writing or demonstrated curiosity about the subject upon which I would write. That was incredibly painful. Never feeling good enough damaged my relationship with myself, other people, and God.

Another result of being abandoned was a racing mind that made it impossible for me to focus and accomplish tasks. My mind jumped around from thought to thought and place to place. I was a skinny boy who had little body fat. My intense nervousness, fear, and anxiety caused me to burn calories while sitting still. Graduating college was a major accomplishment since I was unable to concentrate for any length of time. I could read short articles, but a novel or lengthy book never could hold my attention. But I was good at sports. Because I would obtain affirmation when competing in sports, I loved them all. The constant movement to relieve stress increasingly added to my physical stamina and physique.

My beloved grandmother died when I was eighteen. I was devastated. Shortly after graduating college, I landed a good job and thought myself stable enough to marry. My girlfriend and I agreed to marry after she graduated. Her parents had generously given her a trip to Europe as a graduation gift. While overseas, she became involved with another man and abandoned me. I was devastated. Next to my grandmother, the woman I loved most in the world left me. I experienced too much abandonment to bear. I wanted answers to all this pain and suffering. I sensed that there was a power source similar to the Force from *Star Wars*, a source of power within to help me rise above the circumstances of this world. I set out on a quest to find it.

I started sharing my pain with friends and family. An older woman who knew my pain said my happiness would come from inside me and not from the world. She encouraged me to read philosophy. I had a hunger and craving for knowledge in a variety of subjects. I believed it would fill my mind with more than just existential thoughts. I hoped it would take me into another dimension—the spiritual world. The spiritual world, I sensed, was the true force of the universe. It was powerful.

It was early 1980, my brother Roger shared with me his observations of my life and circumstances. He saw how I depended on other people for my happiness. With this information, I was determined to find this "force" so that I would never again have to rely on another human for happiness. I believed I could own the power of happiness from within. The fear and insecurity I grew up with needed to be conquered with power. The draw to an immense power outside myself filled me with suspense.

I started this journey reading as much philosophy as I could, bringing understanding to my life outside my business realm. There seemed to be something more to life to which I was oblivious. I read Plato, about the Trial of Socrates, Carlos Castenada, Yogananda, Kahlil Gibron, and Ragnish. There was power in the words of these writers as they alluded to the existence of a power and of God. I craved the power so that I could be more than a natural man. I wanted to be a powerful, peaceful man.

After reading these philosophical masters, I was given a small book called *Illusions* by Richard Bach, the author of *Jonathan Livingston Seagull*. The metaphors contained within it deepened my thinking toward an untapped power. As I read *Illusions*, the power of the force increased, and I became excited about living. I sensed that the power was evolving. Curiosity kept driving me as I shared what I was learning with friends. I told them about my deep philosophical thoughts and the power I felt as my way of contributing to the world and overcoming a mundane existence. I was being drawn to God. The theme of all the philosophy I was reading focused on power and peace from within, such as this excerpt from *Illusions:*

> Once there lived a village of creatures along the bottom of a great crystal river. The current of the river swept silently over them all—young and old, rich and poor, good and evil, the current going its own way, knowing only its own crystal self. Each creature in its own manner clung tightly to the twigs and rocks at the river bottom, for clinging was their way of life, and resisting the current what each had learned from birth. But one creature said at last, "I am tired of clinging. Though I cannot see it with my eyes, I trust the current knows where it is going. I shall let go, and let it take me where it will. Clinging, I shall die of boredom." The other creatures

> laughed and said, "Fool! Let go, and that
> current you worship will throw you tumbled
> and smashed across the rocks, and you shall
> die quicker than boredom!" But the one
> heeded them not, and taking a breath did let
> go, and at once was tumbled and smashed
> by the current across the rocks. Yet in time,
> as the creature refused to cling again, the
> current lifted him free from the bottom, and
> he was bruised and hurt no more.[2]

This was the life I was looking for—to be swept by a river, lifted free, bruised and hurt no more. Isaiah, a book in the Bible, says, "When you pass through the waters, I will be with you; and when you pass through the rivers, they will not sweep over you. When you walk through the fire, you will not be burned; the flames will not set you ablaze" (Isaiah 43:2).

I am also reminded of the rivers that surrounded the garden of Eden. The first psalm describes the man who is like a tree planted by streams of water. Better yet, the Lord said to the woman at the well, "Whoever believes in me . . . rivers of living water will flow from within them" (John 7:38).

I gave a copy of *Illusions* to a close colleague at work, and surprisingly, he had great things to say about it. He also told me that some of the thoughts the book contained had been paraphrased from the Bible. Then with deliberate loving-kindness, he asked me if l had ever read the philosophy of the New Testament. My response was no. He suggested I should start with the New Testament if I was going to read the Bible. And just like that, with a simple encouragement to read the philosophy of the New Testament, my trajectory changed.

Around this time, my brother Roger came for a visit. A Christian woman in Texas (where he was living) had given him a New International Version of the Bible that he had been reading while visiting me. When he returned to Texas, he left the Bible behind. There it sat in my living room until my friend encouraged me to read it. I started with Matthew and read through Mark, Luke, and John. I loved it! And yet there were still so many things I could not comprehend. This man Jesus I was reading about had real power; His power was more than that of a mere man. He had power from God. Power to love, heal, change water to wine, walk on water, and more. Wow! This was real power. And yet people wanted Him dead. Why?

I became aroused by my newfound interest in power. I knew the Bible was powerful in some way. God is powerful—I knew that. I wanted to know all He said and about the power I sensed the book contained.

With hungry eyes, I opened the Bible translated in a version that I could somewhat understand. I was amazed at the words speaking truth to me. This was the beginning of a journey. My journey in the study of the Bible has continued for over forty-four years. The Bible still speaks and excites me daily. From that time forward, I have never put it down. It has enthralled me with profound wisdom spoken by Christ. His parables have lured my thoughts as I focused on the meaning behind them.

As I began reading my Bible, I was getting closer to the force for which I had been searching. There was so much of it I did not understand, but I had the desire to learn. In a moment I will never forget, I felt the force of the words strike me to the core of my being. One day, my neighbor and I were drinking beers after work. He rolled a marijuana joint to accompany his beer. Being an athlete I was not a pot smoker; I valued my body. In addition, I had seen the destructive forces that pot had on many of my friends throughout high school. It had truly altered their personalities. I never judged anyone for smoking, but I knew that it was not for me. On this day, however, I changed my mind, and I indulged with my neighbor.

The results were astonishing. My mind slowed down to the point where it was not racing. I was able to focus with intensity, which increased my ability to understand. It was like I was seeing and experiencing a slow-motion world for the first time. Colors were more vivid, and my senses were heightened. I experienced life as an observer rather than a participant. The world was out there at a safe distance. I realized that God had walked the face of the earth, and the power of God could be seen living in and through a human being. My mind started to assess. What if God really had come to visit earth? What was the power He carried with Him through this journey?

With this cathartic safety net, I began incessantly reading philosophy. I found that I could understand every word I was reading, which was a first for me. I had wonderful conversations with friends as I shared some principles I had learned from my reading. When I first started to read the Bible, there was so much I did not comprehend.

Reflecting back on that period of my life, I recognize that I was in a low point, and I didn't care what I was doing to my body. The reason I include this aspect of my story is not to advocate marijuana usage but to emphasize the fact that God will meet us where we are regardless of the circumstances.

The woman who had given Roger the Bible became his bride, and they came to Denver to live. Shortly after their move to Denver, I found myself praying to God for further understanding of the Bible. I asked if He could lead me to a church where they taught the meaning of the Word. Two days later, my new sister-in-law, Debbie, invited me to a church. Debbie told me she and Roger would be visiting a new church on Sunday. She had heard from her friends of a new Christian fellowship that was an offshoot from another Presbyterian church. It was a start-up church, without their own building. To my brother's surprise, I told them I would attend. My prayer had been answered in two days. I knew it was from God, and I was astounded at His timely response.

As I mentioned before, I loved sports of all kinds. Sports were my great escape before I discovered pot. I had spent years on a basketball court and was currently playing every day at the YMCA. My brother and his wife picked me up to attend church. To my amazement, the church met in the gymnasium of a Christian high school. They had rented the space until a building could be funded. I will never forget the words my brother said as we entered the building. At the threshold of the gym, he turned to me and said, "It would take a basketball court to get you into a church."

I was at home in that gym, not realizing I was also coming home to God. The pastor was starting a series on the book of John. I sat in the bleacher section and devoured the words he spoke. His sermon inspired me enough to ask my new girlfriend if she wanted to go with me the following weekend. The very next week, my girlfriend and I sat in the bleachers while the pastor began teaching the book of John. He said he would go verse by verse through the book until he was done, however long that would take. It took him four Sundays to explain the first three verses of John. "In the beginning was the Word, and the Word was with God, and the Word was God. He was with God in the beginning. Through him all things were made; without him nothing was made that has been made" (John 1:1–3).

My girlfriend and I looked at each other as I said, "I didn't know Jesus is God. Did you?" She said no. Mind you, she had attended church for years and is a very bright woman (a lawyer presently). Saying this was an astonishing revelation. I remember being in awe of this. God had walked among us on the face of this earth. How had I not heard of this before? Why was this information not being talked about?

And further yet, I was troubled by what they had done to God. They had nailed Him to a cross. This was awful! The founder and creator of the world and universe allowed Himself to be nailed to a cross. It felt like the epitome of man's inhumanity to man but also man's inhumanity to God. I really needed to think on this. It was a true revelation, even among all the other philosophy

I had been reading. My mind was swirling, and I started reading the Bible with greater understanding. Still, I wrestled with belief. What if it was not true?

Many times in my life, I had been in bad situations. During those times, I had negotiated with God to prove that He was real. God had never let me down when I asked Him to prove Himself. Clearly, I was testing Him.

One specific example was the time I lost my wallet. I was nineteen and on my way to buy a jeep. In my wallet was a two-thousand-dollar cashier's check made out to me, as well as all my identification. I left the wallet on top of a pay phone as I called the owner of the Jeep to say I was on my way.

It took three minutes for me to realize that I had left my wallet behind, and in that time, someone stole it. When my bank would not stop payment on the check, I was totally defeated. I prayed to God for help. The very next day, the Post Office called about my wallet. The thief had taken sixty dollars of my cash and then dropped my wallet in a mailbox. The two-thousand-dollar check was still intact! God was faithful, and I was not. I rationalized this experience as chance.

I'm sure that I am not alone in this. So many times, I asked God for help, received that help, and then rationalized it happened by coincidence. On a Sunday after attending church, I sat at my desk reading the Bible. I had no idea that Jesus was God, that He had visited the earth two thousand years previously, and that He had been crucified, buried, and had come back to life. In all my philosophical reading, I knew there had to be truth, one truth. For a moment, I paused.

I was experiencing a throbbing pain in my left knee from a sports injury and surgery. The surgery had been seven years prior, but I was beginning to lose my range of motion. I had to limp on my left toes because I could not extend my knee. Once again, I was going to test God. I had been reading of all the healings in the Bible that Jesus had performed, and I needed one desperately. I started the negotiation with God and said, "Jesus, if you are real, heal my knee." I fell into the category of people who had seen all of Jesus's miracles but still did not believe.

As I sat negotiating with God, I remembered the words of Jesus. "Do not put the Lord your God to the test" (Mathew 4:7). I realized that in that moment, I was doing just that. I was making my belief in Him conditional on this healing. It was time to decide and end this torment of doubt. Either Jesus was God or the other philosophy I was reading still contained the truth.

As I drew closer to the edge of belief, it was the appearance of Jesus after His death that did it. More than five hundred people witnessed Him in the course of forty days (1 Corinthians 3–8). Wow! Someone had actually died and come back to say, "Cheer up! There is no death." I knew in my heart it could not be both ways. I considered all the other ways God had proven His existence to me, and there I was asking Him to prove it one more time.

As I talked with Christ, I asked why I should believe the Bible and Jesus above any other philosophy. More proof was in His death, burial, and resurrection. No man had ever survived death and come back to life and made it known. "For we know that since Christ was raised from the dead, he cannot die again; death no longer has mastery over him" (Romans 6:9). And Revelation tells us that "'He will wipe every tear from their eyes. There will be no more death' or mourning or crying or pain, for the old order of things has passed away" (Revelation 21:4). That truly is the ultimate power—the power for which I had been searching.

I was going to trust the Man who had come back from the dead. That was enough to convict me. He had proven to me that He was real, and I would no longer doubt His existence. It happened in a flash. So, with that conviction, all I said was, "Okay, Jesus. You are God." I was certain with no doubt.

On November 1, 1981, Jesus gave me baptism in His Holy Spirit. It was a true gift of love and eternal existence with Him. Before this encounter, I had wondered if my life existed as just a mass of cells bumping into other masses of cells. Was there any meaning or purpose to life?

Instantly, I became overwhelmed with the love of God. The Holy Spirit entered me, and I fell on the floor crying. The promise of the Holy Spirit had descended upon me and flooded me with a river of love I had never known. *Why me?* I kept asking Him. *How could You love me so much?* I was brought to my knees in a love relationship with my Lord, and I cried for three solid days because of this overwhelming love. It is a love that has lasted a lifetime. The moment I believed Jesus, I knew the power for which I had been searching had arrived. It was the power of His love that overwhelmed me—the true power of the universe.

I had read in philosophy that there had to be truth, a single truth. I decided this was the truth, and I accepted Him and all the teachings of the Bible. There were many similarities between what I was reading in the Bible and what I had read in philosophy. For example, the Eastern religions would say, "The wanting is in the not wanting." In the Ten Commandments, God said the same thing: you should not covet or want (Exodus 20:17).

At my desk that day, I fell to my knees. I was humbled by the power of love. It was not what I had been expecting. I did not repent of my sins, and I did not ask forgiveness. Instead, my search was in wanting to know God. While I had been searching, He had been persuading me. On that day, He persuaded me and led me to logical conclusions through philosophy and the Bible. I would never be the same again, and I would never deny the existence of God. I was sealed by the Holy Spirit and enveloped in His love forever.

The Holy Spirit sealed me that day and enclosed me in God's unconditional love. My thoughts, actions, and direct communication with God would now be led by the indwelling of the Holy Spirit and not my own volition. "Because the Holy Spirit is the power by which believers come to Christ and see with new eyes of faith, He is closer to us than we are to ourselves. Like the eyes of the body through which we see physical things, He is seldom in focus to be seen directly, because He is the one through whom all else is seen in a new light."[3]

My oldest brother had become a believer of Christ while I was still in college. He had prompted me to read the Bible, which, at the time, I had no time for. Now it was different. Not only did I find the time, but I had the desire. He was the first person with whom I shared the news. In the letter that I wrote him, I explained we were true brothers now—not only biologically, but now we had the same Father in God.

At that moment, I wanted to tell the world of His great love and how, in an instant, He had changed my heart and my sight. He changed how I viewed the world. For the first time, I looked at people and the world with love rather than fear. I had the same eyes, but I was seeing things differently. I realized that God had gotten a very bad rap in the world. I said to Him, "Please let me be your mouthpiece. Let me share You with the world."

It has taken forty-four years for God to mature me to a point of understanding and to share with me what He wants me to say about Him. The first twenty years of my walk were consumed with guilt that had been taught to me in the church. I was trying to look like and be a good Christian, focused on myself and my behavior. I carried the guilt of smoking pot while reading the Bible and attending church. So many times, I tried to quit smoking pot because I was consumed by the guilt. In one frustrated moment, I told my sister that I wanted to stop smoking pot.

Her reply was, "You won't stop on your own. Only God living in and through you will make it stop."

"What does that look like?" I asked. She did not know the answer. The Christian world struggles with the same question. How? God allowed a twenty-year wrestling match to take place within me so that I could learn of His power, His love, and how to deal with sin in my life. To be free. My walk started with being consumed in His love, but the Church taught me how to be consumed in my guilt and sin.

If you can relate with this, please read on. The answers are in the Bible, and I hope that both my voice and His voice can open your heart to the true power of God, which is love. Love is the most amazing power in the universe. There is never enough said about the love of God in the Christian community. The focus among believers becomes confession of sin and guilt, leading to the condemnation of believers. God does not beat you down with the conviction of sin and guilt. We bring that on ourselves. I would never want a God that I believed in to pile on condemnation and guilt. Most humans already feel bad about themselves.

I cried when I read where Philip says, "Lord, show us the Father and that will be enough for us" (John 14:8). Jesus responded, "Don't you know me, Philip, even after I have been among you such a long time? Anyone who has seen me has seen the Father" (John 14:9). I wept as I read this because I had been like Philip, all the time doubting. I could feel the loneliness of our Lord, as I believed that nobody understood who He really was. God walked the face of our earth full of love, kindness, and healing. He encountered doubt even from Peter, who knew who He was. Peter denied Him three times in fear of his life (Luke 22:54–60). I still weep when I think of how alone He must have felt. I weep as I think about how totally misunderstood He was. This misunderstanding is still going on through the misinterpretation of His words.

After forty-four years, I am still learning who He is. He is God after all, and I could never compare His thoughts to my thoughts. Why would I want to? No greater love, acceptance, and wisdom have I ever marveled at. His grace is overwhelming. What immense patience God has with me.

I share now my understanding of Him. This is what I asked for: to be a mouthpiece and speak for Him. Forty-four years have passed, and I am finally ready to talk, in a big way, about His love. His gift of eternal life is larger than anyone can imagine. I am here to tell of what I know and to praise God and honor Him with these words, to strengthen others in their faith and loose the bonds of slavery to sin and guilt, which has very little do with God's love. Sin and guilt are Satan's stronghold in the Church today. They are what keeps believers from being all they can be.

It is this continued confessing of sins that absolutely destroyed my relationship with Christ for twenty-two years. This is what most Christian churches believe and follow. The conclusion a person would have to draw from this confessing sin is that we are never forgiven of this sin issue in our life. On the other hand, this same group of Christians will tell you that God loves you and has forgiven all your sins. This teaching of constant condemnation of sin and guilt drove me insane and distanced me from Christ. This is the way the Church as an institution has evolved, by using religion to control the congregation.

God help us all if we do not have the sin and guilt to go with our walk in the Lord. God help us all if we do not have pastors preaching sin and guilt from the pulpit. In some way, they believe if you are free from sin and guilt, you will lose control like the people of Israel who were led out of Egypt and built a golden calf to be their god (Exodus 32). At the base of the mountain of God, they started a rebellion and a celebration of lawlessness in defiance of the covenant to follow God.

The Church today believes you will do the same if you aren't driven by sin and guilt. You will not live up to the call of holiness. Pastors are to assist you in becoming more holy, and you should never consider yourself free from the bondage of sin or be declared holy. Christ accomplished both of these things on the cross. But you wouldn't know this if you listen to the ignorance of our modern-day Church.

I refute these teachings because I love people and wish them to rise to new levels of love and understanding in Christ. I refute all the churches who start their worship service with the confession of sin. How absurd. Many pastors today remind me of used car salesmen. They don't really know what the car is capable of, what its reliability is, or what the needs of the customer are. They are motivated either by promises of blessings or by the fear of damnation and not by the love of God, which should be enough to sell and maintain a congregation. I must admit that for the first twenty years of my walk, I bought into this sort of belief.

So, onward Christian soldiers! Let's explore the battleground—the mind—together!

Reflection Questions

1. What is your story? What elements of your past influence and impacted the present?

2. How did your family assist or hinder you on your journey toward God?

3. Who speaks into your life to keep directing you toward God?

4. Are there areas of pain from your past that you are willing to let God heal?

2

THE JOURNEY
CONTINUES

After acknowledging Jesus is God and having been struck with His tremendous love and understanding, the world appeared different. Light penetrated the darkness, and I had increased understanding and compassion toward others. I could not wait to share my faith, and I would pray each day that God would bring three new people to me with whom I could share the love of God. I was parroting what the Church had taught me, not fully knowing what I was talking about. I was high on Jesus and felt as if I were walking three feet off the ground—all was good.

Christians in my church warned me that my bliss would not last. I was shocked at the discouragement they sent my way, but I was not disheartened. I joined the singles ministry at our church and loved the group interaction and support.

My business was taking off, and I saw the hand of God working in all I was doing. Nothing was transpiring by happenstance. Life had become much easier with my newfound love for God. I made good choices, worked harder than normal, felt energized, and was ready to take on the world. With God's help, I truly felt I could do anything. When I got stuck, I would ask God what to do, and answers and affirmations would come. Being immersed in the love of God, I became more loving, generous, and patient.

After two years, bad choices started to emerge in my walk with God. As I spiraled, the guilt and shame were overwhelming. I became a prodigal son. I married, having dated for only two months and with sexual lust leading the way. I sold the equipment in my paving business, but rather than pay off the debt, I squandered the money by not working. My dad's name was on the debt, and the disappointment I caused him was immense.

My dad's second wife was not pleased by my actions and hired lawyers to sue me. She and my dad did not need the money, nor was the debt of any consequence to them. She simply pursued a lawsuit because she didn't like me. Five lawyers hired by my dad's wife started proceedings against me, but each dropped the case. None of the lawyers felt comfortable with the idea of a father suing his son.

I started over. My wife had filed for divorce, and I was living in the basement of a friend's house with one month of free rent. I was broken. The most humbling aspect of all, however, was that I started attending the singles group of my church again. They all had full knowledge that I had been married for only three months. None of them shamed me, but I carried it inside.

In this singles group, I was blessed to meet a Christian psychologist named Michael. He was lecturing on a book, *The Road Less Traveled*, by M. Scott Peck. The content was good, and I was drawn to Michael. I was stuck in life and felt there was no light ahead. At the end of the lecture, I asked for his card and made an appointment.

My first session with Michael was filled with love and understanding. He listened to the story of my prodigal journey, and at the end of our session, he asked me these questions.

"Do you love God?"

I said, "Very much."

"Does God love you?"

"Without a doubt," I answered.

"You don't love what God made you to be, but I can help," he said. He laid out the groundwork of meeting together once a week. I was so eager to receive understanding and freedom that I pushed to meet twice a week. He agreed and even gave me a discount. I will be forever grateful. I sold my Porsche and bought a clunker, so I could pay for therapy, restart my paving business, and start fresh in my life.

I never lost the love of God, and I read the Word daily. With the God-directed help of a friend and hard work I eventually paid off my business debt. Through therapy, I gained freedom to speak the thoughts I had been hiding, which accelerated my healing. As I released my hold on defense mechanisms, my heart began to fill with motivation to accept myself. My walk with the Lord tightened as I depended on Him more.

In my therapy sessions, I did not face the truth and the darkness of my ways alone. God was always with me. Miracle after miracle came my way. God never turned His back on me, regardless of all the trials and tribulations. I started to understand more deeply the words of the Bible as I went through therapy and self-examination. Jesus said,

> "Why do you look at the speck of sawdust
> in your brother's eye and pay no attention
> to the plank in your own eye? How can you

> say to your brother, 'Let me take the speck
> out of your eye,' when all the time there is a
> plank in your own eye? You hypocrite, first
> take the plank out of your own eye, and then
> you will see clearly to remove the speck from
> your brother's eye" (Matthew 7:3–5).

I found His words to be true. The depth at which I looked at my feelings, emotions, actions, and thoughts seemed to be the depth I could see into others. The ability to express my thoughts, regardless of how bizarre they were, led me on a journey of discovery. This freedom to speak whatever I thought ended up strengthening my relationship with God. With Michael's unconditional acceptance, I was able to experience more of God's acceptance.

I used to tell Michael how sad it was that people have to pay other people to listen to them. The Bible says that we should "carry each other's burdens, and in this way you will fulfill the law of Christ" (Galatians 6:2). Not many people in my life have been able to meet what Paul describes as the law of Christ.

The concepts of transference and projection are much of why psychotherapy is effective. Our emotions don't have eyes or logic, but they are what we feel. That's why we can view a movie and cry or laugh. Michael, as a male authority figure, brought up buried feelings I was holding for my father.

One day while I was speaking my thoughts in therapy, I was particularly angry with my dad. I envisioned myself with a bullwhip, striking Michael's back. I was transferring the anger I felt with my dad onto Michael. In an instant, my vision of Michael suffering because of my whip turned to a vision of Jesus on the cross. I was astonished and amazed. Michael willingly stayed with me and allowed me to transfer and project my feelings onto him so that I could heal. In the same way, Jesus allows us to transfer sin onto Him so that we can heal and be restored to our Father God.

That process healed me of my anger toward my dad, and that healing helped reconcile our relationship. It also brought a greater understanding and appreciation for the love of Jesus and how He healed all mankind. A few years later, my dad was diagnosed with cancer. In his final days, God blessed our relationship with closeness, honesty, and a genuine love for each other. Knowing his time was short, my dad chose to die in my newly purchased house instead of a hospital.

As his body failed him and death approached, he slipped into an unconscious state. Unable to respond, I knew he could hear every word I was saying. Late in the evening, I held his head in my hands and asked him to go toward the bright light in front of him, God's love waiting for him. To my astonishment, he stopped breathing. As I held him, an electrical pulse went through me with such strength that I had to release my hold on him. I walked with my dad to the edge of eternity and delivered him into the love of the Lord. I was elated because I saw it as a birth, not a death. This experience became the crown jewel of my life. The love of God blessed and touched a father and son.

During this season, I was still conflicted regarding what the role sin and guilt played in my walk with the Lord. The love of God spurred me on, but the conflict of sin and guilt remained. I read in one of John's letters that "everyone who makes a practice of sinning also practices lawlessness; sin is lawlessness. You know that he appeared in order to take away sins, and in him there is no sin. No one who abides in him keeps on sinning; no one who keeps on sinning has either seen him or known him" (1 John 3:4–6 ESV). This passage touched my heart deeply.

I loved God, but at times I made a practice of sinning. I felt horrible when I read verses like these. I needed a revelation about this because I knew that I was going to sin the rest of my life. As I experienced this wrestling match, the guilt I was feeling from sinning drove me further away from God. His persuasion never left me, and I was always aware of Him being with me.

The wrestling match changed after 9/11. I was tuning into the AM radio channels trying to glean information. One day, I stumbled upon a very kind and gentle voice talking about Jesus. This pastor, Colin Cook, was delivering a message that I had not heard before. It sounded close to blasphemy. He was talking about including God in our sins—even to the point of praising Him while we're sinning.

In twenty years of walking with God, I had never heard anything like this. He stated God uses sin in our lives to draw us closer to Him. My attention was piqued. I wanted to be closer to God, but I felt distant from Him because of the sin in my life. I felt like Jacob wrestling with God (Genesis 32:22-31). Jacob did not let go of God until he was blessed. This became the blessing to me.

The reason we can include God in our sin is because "there is therefore now no condemnation for those who are in Christ Jesus" (Romans 8:1 ESV). This was the assurance I needed. I focused on this verse, especially the words "no condemnation." The verse felt freeing and much like the therapy I had experienced with Michael. I was given permission to think and say all I wanted to with God and praise Him that He would never leave me. I could include God in my conscious sinning—whether I followed through with it or not—and praise Him. In time, the thoughts of sinning only reminded me that I never left the presence of my loving God.

Now it all made sense. God could not help me if I excluded Him from anything in my life, even if it was sinful. Eventually, I realized that the sin that had been against me now reminded me of God and strengthened me instead. I focused on God and His unconditional acceptance alongside my thoughts of sin. My awareness of the overriding love of God took the sting out of sin. I was not confessing sin, guilt, or remorse. Rather, I was praising God, which was a piercing understanding and revelation.

With this newfound love in God, I really started to examine Scripture. While studying the Bible, I kept running across the word *sin*. With my newfound understanding of praising God in sin, I began to see a different interpretation of the Word of God. Jesus told the adulterous woman who was being stoned to go and sin no more (see John 8:1–11). That never made sense to me. Not one of us in this body of flesh can sin no more. Why would Jesus assign a task impossible to carry out?

I wrestled with this concept until I received a revelation about the word *sin*. God was showing me how sin was mostly in unbelief, not in the transgressions of the commandments. When Jesus said, "Go and sin no more," He was telling the lady to set aside her unbelief in God. Jesus touched her with love, acceptance, and understanding. He gave her reason to believe in God by loving her. Through the woman's belief in Jesus, she would be declared righteous before God and sanctified in Christ. She would indeed sin no more. As I understood this concept, relief filled me with the love of God I had experienced twenty years earlier. Jesus allowed this struggle, and I had found peace. The wrestling match was over; the blessing was to rest in Him.

Reflection Questions

1. What is your initial experience with God's love? How did that change your perspective on life?

2. What has been your experience when you needed someone to listen? Were they able to listen without giving advice?

3. Describe any encounters with Jesus or others that have influenced your understanding of forgiveness and reconciliation.

4. What is your view of sin? Has it changed based off of what this chapter taught?

3

SIN AND HOW TO DEAL
WITH IT

The topic of sin has always perplexed me. As a Christian, it is obviously something I do not desire, yet it happens. Violation of God's law in word, thought, or deed is a sin. This is an impossible standard. No man has achieved this—except Jesus. God's original design of man did not include sin.

Your life can be changed forever when you believe that the true message of God is love, grace, and life. The synopsis of the entire Bible can be summarized by Jesus's words: "Love the Lord your God with all your heart and with all your soul and with all your mind and with all your strength" (Mark 12:30). Assured in His love and Spirit, you can love your neighbor as yourself. It is a simple message that has gone astray as men have tried to control their own behavior, which results in them trying to control the behavior of others.

Guilt can be a massive driver toward the desire to control. We struggle to maintain control in out-of-control situations by blaming ourselves. When situations arise, self-blame can become a coping mechanism and a way to understand the situations. It is a way of thinking that cannot easily be sustained living in an out-of-control world. Oddly, we can interpret our guilt as a safe place to harvest control. God freed us from guilt:

> You, my brothers and sisters, were called to be free. But do not use your freedom to indulge the flesh; rather, serve one another humbly in love. For the entire law is fulfilled in keeping this one command: "Love your neighbor as yourself." If you bite and devour each other, watch out or you will be destroyed by each other. (Galatians 5:13–15)

THE ISSUE OF SIN

I have counseled Christians of every age who still struggle with sin and shame despite their bravest efforts to overcome. Most Christians are holding on to a belief that causes them never to experience hope in their faith. The world and the Christian faith have distorted who

God is and what He expects from us. We are taught to live under the pressure of performance—producing results and changing ourselves.

No sin has more severity than another in the eyes of God. The wages of just one sin, any sin, is death (Romans 6:23). And James tells us, "For the person who keeps all of the laws except one is as guilty as a person who has broken all of God's laws" (James 2:10 NLT). God also states that we are born into this condition. For the human race, sin is the natural state of being. In the Fall, God commanded Adam and Eve not to eat from the tree of the knowledge of good and evil, warning them that they would die if they did. When they disobeyed, "sin entered the world through one man, and death through sin, and in this way death came to all people, because all sinned" (Romans 5:12).

The issue of sin is the main topic of belief in the Christian world, as all men are condemned to death by God because of sin. This is why we have need of a Savior in Christ Jesus; He came to give us life. "The wages of sin is death, but the gift of God is eternal life in Christ Jesus" (Romans 6:23). Sin is the symptom that leads to the main problem of death and separation from God.

The righteous standing of man before God always comes through faith. Abraham, the firstborn of the Jews, believed God and was credited with righteousness

(Romans 4:3). That is to say that Abraham had right standing with God based on one thing: belief or faith in God. That hasn't changed throughout all of history. It is by faith alone we have right standing before God. The Old Testament sacrificial system was to enhance relationship with God. It made the Hebrew people aware of their faith in the present, and it pointed them to the Messiah who was to come.

God has always been a forgiving God. Seldom has sin separated man from God. Separation has only occurred because of our unbelief, or our lack of faith and love toward God. Even at the Fall of Adam and Eve, God pursued them as they hid from Him in shame and guilt. He comforted them with an animal sacrifice, covering their sin, never breaking relationship with them.

Ours is an even greater relationship without a sin covering because sin has been taken away, once and for all: "Look, the Lamb of God, who takes away the sin of the world!" (John 1:29). Jesus was naked and without a covering while hanging on the cross, accepting the sin of world. We have a comforting God who is always in pursuit of us, and we respond to Him in faith and belief. The constant, never-changing, always-loving God of the ages.

REMOVAL OF THE CURSE

The greatest news in the history of man came when Christ removed this curse of sin and death. He offered Himself and His life to reconcile us back to a permanent relationship with God. What I object to in the Christian faith is the guilt associated with this act of love in reconciling us to God. I recently heard a pastor say that we hung Jesus on the cross. It would seem he failed to read John 10:17–18, which states:

> "The reason my Father loves me is that I lay down my life—only to take it up again. No one takes it from me, but I lay it down of my own accord. I have authority to lay it down and authority to take it up again. This command I received from my Father."

In the Christian realm, there always seems to be a motivation of guilt and sin that is associated with knowing God. Yet, Isaiah says, "It was the LORD's will to crush him and cause him to suffer" (Isaiah 53:10).

How can we be completely forgiven but then have to confess and ask forgiveness? All was accomplished in Christ on the cross. There is no forgiveness of sin without the shedding of blood. If confessing sin is about forgiveness, why did Christ have to die? If confession is what keeps us in good standing with God, then confession usurps the power of the cross and what Jesus accomplished.

Sanctification is the process of God's grace by which the believer is separated from sin and becomes dedicated to God in His righteousness.

> "Sacrifices and offerings, burnt offerings and sin offering you did not desire, nor were you pleased with them"—though they were offered in accordance with the law. Then he said, "Here I am, I have come to do your will." He sets aside the first to establish the second. And by that will, we have been made holy through the sacrifice of the body of Jesus Christ once for all. (Hebrews 10:8–10)

We are set apart by God, made holy by the sacrifice of Christ. You will never become more holy than the day you first believed in Christ. Holiness is not in you. It is in Christ, and when you accept and believe in Him, it's in you through Him. Noah was placed in an ark and passed through the waters of God's judgment. The one and only door of the ark was sealed by God when Noah and his family entered. That process is a picture of how the one and only Christ accomplished the same for us. We have entered the body of Christ, sealed by His Holy Spirit. "For by one offering he hath perfected forever them that are sanctified" (Hebrews 10:14 ASV).

There are many versions of the Bible that added we are "being sanctified," never to rest in the accomplished work of Jesus. Somehow, we work our way toward sanctification and holiness. This belief is an abomination of God's Word.

ALWAYS SINFUL

The destructive force in confession of sin and asking forgiveness stems from a gross misinterpretation of 1 John 1:9. The word *sin* has a few meanings. It can mean a violation of God's law, both willful and unwilful; however, it also can mean unbelief.

> Strong's Concordance 266 *hamartía* – feminine noun derived from /A "not" and 3313 /*méros*, "a part, share of")—properly, no share ("no part of"); loss (forfeiture) because of not hitting *the target*, sin, (*missing the mark*).

> *Hamartía* ("sin, forfeiture because missing the mark") is the brand of sin that emphasizes its *self*-originated (*self*-empowered) nature— i.e. it is not originated or empowered by God (i.e. *not of faith*, His inworked persuasion, cf. Ro 14:23).

When we view these definitions, we should see that the focus is on God and faith. When we don't have God, our only option is self-empowerment. But when we have God in our lives, self-empowerment should have no part of our living process. The reference to Romans 14:23 deals with faith, and anything apart from faith is sin.

I first learned of sin and its definition early in my walk. I was told that sin means to miss the mark, such as an archer missing a target. I wasn't sure, however, what the target was. If I make the commandments the target, where is God? The commandments and rituals of the Hebrew nation were the target in the time of Christ. They missed the true target by not recognizing the Messiah among them. The most destructive misinterpretation of the Bible comes from 1 John 1:5–10 (ASV):

> And this is the message which we have heard from him and announce unto you, that God is light, and in him is no darkness at all. If we say we have fellowship with him and walk in the darkness, we lie, and do not practice the truth: but if we walk in the light, as he is in the light, we have fellowship with one another, and the blood of Jesus his Son cleanses us from all sin. If we say that we have no sin, we deceive ourselves, and the truth is not in us. If we confess our sins, he is faithful and righteous to forgive us our sins, and to cleanse us from all unrighteousness. If we say that we have not sinned, we make him a liar, and his word is not in us.

I believe this is the great contributor of guilt in the Christian life. If we have to continually confess our sins, then God is still holding something against us. The word *confess* appears at least ten times in the New Testament and is the confession of faith, or the lack thereof. An example is found in the apostle John's second letter: "For many deceivers have gone out into the world, those who do not confess the coming of Jesus Christ in the flesh. Such a one is the deceiver and the antichrist" (2 John 1:7 ESV).

John is addressing Gnostics who had entered the ranks of early believers in Christ; however, Gnostics did not believe Jesus had come in a physical body. The Gnostics believed the earth realm and the physical body was evil. They believed that the way to salvation was knowledge, which would release their spirit. These were the apostates that had infiltrated the early believers.

I do not wish to spend time discussing this false belief, but much of Gnosticism has been resurrected in the New Age movement of our modern era. As Solomon wrote, there is nothing new under the sun (Ecclesiastes 1:9). Many false teachings grew in popularity in the first century. Paul warned of this: "See to it that no one takes you captive through hollow and deceptive philosophy, which depends on human tradition and the elemental spiritual forces of this world rather than on Christ" (Colossians 2:8).

Another warning comes from Timothy: "The Spirit clearly says that in later times some will abandon the faith and follow deceiving spirits and things taught by demons. Such teachings come through hypocritical liars, whose consciences have been seared as with a hot iron" (1 Timothy 4:1–2).

The problem in 1 John 1:5–10 is the definition of sin. In the Gospel of John, Jesus tells us the definition of sin: "When he [the Advocate] comes, he will prove the world to be in the wrong about sin and righteousness and judgment: about sin, because people do not believe in me; about righteousness, because I am going to the Father, where you can see me no longer" (John 16:8–10). The Spirit, or Helper, will convict the world of sin because men do not believe in Jesus.

The apostle John wrote the book of John and is fully aware of what Jesus said. Sin is unbelief, because Jesus took away the sin of the world. "He is the propitiation for our sins, and not for ours only but also for the sins of the whole world" (1 John 2:2 ESV). If the sin of the whole world is forgiven, what remains? Only one sin: unbelief in Jesus, just as he stated in John 16.

Here is the problem with 1 John 1:5–10: the author is addressing both unbelievers and believers, whereas the Gospel of John is written to the unbeliever only. "Jesus performed many other signs in the presence of his disciples, which are not recorded in this book. But these are written that you may believe that Jesus is the Messiah, the Son of God, and that by believing you may have life in his name" (John 20:30–31).

The passage in 1 John starts with the affirmation that Jesus came in the flesh, stating that we have heard, seen, and touched Him. This is clearly addressing the Gnostics. He also states that he is writing so they, too, will have fellowship because, apparently, they are not in fellowship. He goes on to say this is a message we hear from Him and proclaim or declare to you. I believe the second letter of John to be written before the first letter, with this opening defense of Jesus coming in the flesh. It is the defense against the many deceivers and a warning not to be influenced by these false teachers, leading them away from the teachings of Christ.

John goes on to say that if we claim to have fellowship with Him and yet walk in darkness, we lie and do not practice the truth (1 John 1:6). Walking in darkness and not practicing the truth is unbelief, which is the theme of 1 John. I believe the personal pronouns were mixed into the text from you to we and us. If we say we have no sin, then the truth is not in us (or you). If the truth is not in us, again, it is unbelief. If we confess our sin (or unbelief), He is faithful and just to forgive us our sins and cleanse us from all unrighteousness.

From the beginning to the end of the Bible, faith is what declares us righteous. John is declaring a cleansing from unbelief to belief. If we say we have not sinned or have not believed, we make Him out to be a liar, and His word is not in us. Once again, John is stating that an unbelieving person is making God to be a liar, without the word.

The overwhelming evidence that the sin mentioned is the sin of unbelief becomes apparent in the fifth chapter. He reiterates this same message: "He that believeth on the Son of God hath the witness in himself: he that believeth not God hath made him a liar; because he believeth not the record [word] that God gave of his Son" (1 John 5:10 KJV). This closing statement of John is almost exactly the same as the opening in chapter 1. One who does not believe or have faith has made God a liar, and the Word of God is not in him.

John is writing to both believers and unbelievers so that they might share fellowship and life eternal. This is not about confessing our sins and being cleansed from all unrighteousness. There is only one thing and one thing only that cleanses us from all unrighteousness: belief in

Jesus, the Son of the living God. Nowhere else in the New Testament is there confession of sins. Paul wrote two-thirds of the New Testament, and not once does he state that believers must confess their sins. As a Pharisee and follower of the law, Paul most certainly would have written of this if it had been important.

James states, "Therefore confess your sins to each other and pray for each other so that you may be healed. The prayer of a righteous person is powerful and effective" (James 5:16). I would encourage this practice, as it is truly a way in which we heal and overpower sin. We should confess to one another without condemnation because we all sin and fall short of the glory of God (Romans 3:23). If we would share more of ourselves and our shortcomings with each other without condemnation, we would become healthier and happier individuals. We are to bear each other's burdens and so fulfill the law of Christ (Galatians 6:2).

The only thing that stands between us and God is belief or faith. Jesus made it so simple to come to God as you see here in Paul's letter to the Romans:

> "The word is near you, in your mouth and in
> your heart" (that is, the word of faith that we
> proclaim); because if you confess with your
> mouth that Jesus is Lord and believe in your
> heart that God raised him from the dead,

> you will be saved. For with the heart one
> believes and is justified, and with the mouth
> one confesses and is saved. For the Scripture
> says, "Everyone who believes in him will not
> be put to shame." For there is no distinction
> between Jew and Greek; for the same Lord is
> Lord of all, bestowing his riches on all who
> call on him. For "everyone who calls on the
> name of the Lord will be saved." (Romans
> 10:8–13 ESV)

The world has been forgiven. It is all-inclusive, and the only sin remaining in the world is the sin of unbelief. Additionally note how the word *confess* is used to demonstrate belief. The will of God is that all should have salvation and life eternal. God's plan is that He would pay the price for sin. This was God's act of love to redeem us.

I love God and appreciate this great sacrifice. Guilt isn't a motivator to bring me to this all-loving, all-consuming God. We are not to show contempt for the "riches of his kindness, forbearance and patience . . . God's kindness is intended to lead you to repentance" (Romans 2:4). And John reminds us that "God so loved the world that he gave his one and only Son, that whoever believes in him shall not perish but have eternal life. For God did not send his Son into the world to condemn the world, but to save the world through him" (John 3:16–17). Again,

"He is the atoning sacrifice for our sins, and not only for ours but also for the sins of the whole world" (1 John 2:2).

THE SLAVES OF SIN

Throughout history, Christians have often found themselves trapped in a state of bondage, even though Jesus has already paid the price for their sins. This paradox can be seen as a reflection of the Israelites' experience in Egypt. When God led the Hebrew nation out of slavery and bondage in Egypt, they complained to God about their journey of faith. He was leading them to freedom. They were afraid they were going to die in the wilderness and doubted God, and so they proclaimed they wanted to go back to the slavery and bondage in Egypt.

Because of their complaining, lack of faith, and desire to go back to bondage, God kept them aware of their sin and unbelief. He required the very best of their herds as sacrifice to this debt, and He held them in this bondage until the time of Jesus. It may also be viewed as a test of their faith. Christ was the ultimate freedom from the bondage of sin and guilt.

Just as the Israelites were physically liberated from slavery but struggled to embrace their freedom (mentally and spiritually), Christians sometimes find it challenging to fully embrace the freedom and forgiveness that Christ's sacrifice offers. Somehow, we think that we must work for it because we're told there is no free ride.

Just as the Israelites became accustomed to the oppressive and degrading conditions of slavery, Christians can develop a mindset of bondage due to their past sins and guilt. Even though they have accepted Jesus as their Savior, they may continue to dwell on their past mistakes and feel unworthy of God's love and grace.

I was in a Bible study with a man who drove a bus throughout the day. While driving, he would confess all his past sins to make sure none were unconfessed. This lingering guilt can lead to a self-imposed bondage that prevents people from fully experiencing the freedom and abundant life that Christ offers.

Moreover, just as the Israelites faced various challenges and obstacles during their journey to the promised land, Christians can encounter struggles and temptations that hinder their spiritual growth and from fully embracing their freedom. They may find themselves entangled in the same sins for which Christ has already died. This cycle of sin and guilt can create a sense of bondage and frustration, leaving Christians feeling trapped and unable to live in the victory that Christ has won for them. Our struggles with sin should only remind us of who we are

in Christ—not of our guilt. Pastor and Bible teacher
William R. Newell in his commentary on Romans says
this about chapter 6:

> Verse 7: For he that hath died hath been
> declared righteous from sin! We must
> seize fast hold of this blessed verse. Let us
> distinguish at once between being justified
> from sins—from the guilt thereof—by the
> blood of Christ, and being justified from
> *sin*—the thing itself. "Justified from sin"
> is the key to both Chapters Six and Seven
> and also Eight! It is the consciousness of
> being sinful that keeps back saints from that
> glorious life Paul lived. Paul shows absolutely
> no sense of bondage before God; but goes on
> in blessed triumph! Why? He knew he had
> been justified *from all guilt* by the blood of
> Christ; and he knew that he was also justified,
> cleared, from *the thing sin itself* and therefore
> (though walking in an, as yet, unredeemed
> body), he was *wholly heavenly* in his standing,
> life and relations with God! He knew he was
> as really justified from *sin itself* as from *sins*.
> The conscious presence of sin in his flesh
> only reminded him that he was *in Christ*,—
> that sin had been *condemned judicially*, as
> connected with flesh, at the cross; and that
> he was *justified* as to sin; because he had died
> with Christ, and his former relationship to
> sin had *wholly ceased!* Its presence gave him
> no thought of condemnation, but only

eagered his longing for the redemption body.
"Justified from sin"—because, "he that hath
died is justified from sin." Glorious fact! May
we have faith to enter into it as did Paul![1]

Sin becomes bondage when the focus is on the
transgression rather than praising an awesome, loving
God. Trying not to sin becomes the obsession. God wants
us to be obsessed with Him. Real change takes place in a
loving relationship. God places His thoughts in our mind
through the indwelling of the Holy Spirit and reading
His Word. Desiring God places His desires in us.

The fear and doubt the Israelites felt in the wilderness,
the attitude of wanting to stay in bondage, is much the
same today. Christians are still asking for the forgiveness
of sin, as if there is still a debt to be paid and God is
holding something against them. They are unaware that
they are baptized into the death of Christ, buried with
Him, and resurrected with Him. I always ask my Bible
study groups, If you are dead in Christ, how does a dead
person keep on sinning?

THE SIN OF UNBELIEF

I often wonder where this condemnation of sin and
guilt came from. In Jesus's day, did thousands of people
follow Him because they felt guilty? Did they seek Him

because Christ was preaching hellfire and damnation? He brought people to Himself through loving-kindness and compassion; that's the God I know and love. The miracles Christ performed tended to convince people that He knew a loving God who was willing to heal their physical and mental problems.

God's message is not of judgment for misbehaving. The fault He finds is in our unbelief, as it has always been: "Whoever believes in him is not condemned, but whoever does not believe stands condemned already because they have not believed in the name of God's one and only Son" (John 3:18).

Unbelief is a significant spiritual obstacle that hinders our relationship with God and undermines the foundation of our faith. Hebrews warns us about the deceitfulness of unbelief: "See to it, brothers and sisters, that none of you has a sinful, unbelieving heart that turns away from the living God" (Hebrews 3:12). Unbelief undermines the foundation of faith and rejects God's truth. It blinds us to the evidence of God's existence, His love, and His redemptive work. The apostle Paul reminds us that the unbelieving Jews "were broken off because of unbelief," and he warns us to "stand by faith. Do not be arrogant, but tremble" (Romans 11:20).

Unbelief is not merely a lack of knowledge or understanding; it is a deliberate choice to suppress or reject God's truth. It prevents us from experiencing the transformative power of God's grace and restricts His work in our lives. Recognizing and repenting for the sin of unbelief is essential for our relationship and reconciliation to God. By embracing God's truth, seeking Him with an open heart, and nurturing a deep trust in Him, we can overcome the sin of unbelief and experience the abundant life and blessings that come through faith.

What John the Baptist prophesied about Jesus's mission summarizes this point: "Look, the Lamb of God, who takes away the sin of the world!" Jesus declared His mission complete while on the cross (John 19:30). At that moment, God stopped counting people's sins against them. "God was reconciling the world to himself in Christ, not counting people's sins against them. And he has committed to us the message of reconciliation" (2 Corinthians 5:19).

Individual sins no longer separate God from His people. I have heard so many Christians say that God turns His back on them when they sin. Since it is impossible for us to stop sinning, He sent Jesus to be the remedy for sin. Faith in Christ is not the absence of sin; it is life in Him, being led by His Spirit in a world far from God and steeped in a sinful nature. "For those who are led by the Spirit of God are the children of God. The

Spirit you received does not make you slaves, so that you live in fear again; rather, the Spirit you received brought about your adoption to sonship. And by him we cry, '*Abba*, Father'" (Romans 8:14–15).

Jesus tells us the Holy Spirit, whom the Father would send in His name, is to be our advocate. He would teach us all things and remind us of everything He has said to us (John 14:26). What does an advocate do? The word *advocate* comes from the Greek word *parakletos,* which means "one who pleads another's cause, who helps another by defending or comforting him."[2] The Holy Spirit works with believers to defend and comfort them. His job is not to help believers meet God's expectations. His job is to remind believers that Jesus met God's expectations for them.

ISOLATION AND CONDEMNATION

The phrase *love conquers all* is one I take very seriously. Love is the greatest force in the universe. It is the force that binds hearts together and brings healing and life. I have seen the conquering effects of love, specifically in dealing with mental disturbances, both in myself and in others. This force, however, comes from God. There is one who loves us unconditionally, and He is committed to conquering all that is not love. Love conquers all because God is love, and He has already conquered all things—including sin and death.

Year after year, self-help books on overcoming mental health and motivational issues are some of the most popular. The irony is people cannot help themselves; there are no self-made people. We all need other people. God made us relational because He is relational. We see the fact that God is relational when He says, "Let us make mankind in our image, in our likeness" (Genesis 1:26). The us being the Father, Son, and Holy Spirit.

Living life in isolation is a recipe for disaster, a source of defeat. Isolation can exacerbate feelings of anger, frustration, and social disconnection, which may increase the likelihood of violent behavior. Humans have an inherent need for social connection and belonging, and when this need is unmet, it leads to feelings of loneliness and despair.

Most people who commit murder, either of themselves or others, do so because of one major problem: isolation.[3] Numerous other problems stem from isolation including drug and alcohol abuse. We are made to be in relationships, and yet some people choose isolation. Why is that? Condemnation. When one feels condemned, it creates in them a sense of separation and exclusion. Feeling unworthy, ashamed, and judged can lead people to withdraw and isolate as a way to protect their vulnerable sense of self.

Condemnation can erode self-esteem and self-confidence, further contributing to isolation. The cycle of condemnation and isolation is self-perpetuating. The more isolated individuals become, the more they dwell on their perceived flaws or mistakes. Condemnation and guilt are the keys that drive people into isolation. And yet there are churches that teach condemnation from the pulpit, rather than the unconditional love and acceptance of God.

I have found the only safe haven is in my relationship with God. "He will never leave you nor forsake you" (Deuteronomy 31:8). Many have said that Romans 8 is the apex of the Bible.[4] It starts out saying "there is now no condemnation for those who are in Christ" and ends with saying that nothing, "neither height nor depth, nor anything else in all creation, will be able to separate us from the love of God" (Romans 8:39). In the middle of the chapter, we learn that "in all things God works for the good of those who love him" (Romans 8:28).

Where did this message of the love and acceptance of God get lost? The whole of the Bible was summed up by Christ in revealing the most important commandments: love God and love others (Matthew 22:37–39). Loving God and loving others is the key to loving yourself.

Reflection Questions

1. Can you put into words what your belief system is regarding your role in Christianity?

2. Are there ways you find yourself pushing harder and striving for God's approval?

3. What is the God you follow like? Is He angry? Is He loving? What character traits does He have?

4. What Scripture verse mentioned in this chapter jumped out to you? Why?

4

PERSUASION, HEARING, AND WORSHIP

*U*nderstanding the word *faith* opened my mind to massive thoughts about our Lord and how really big and wonderful He is. I was shocked by the definition of this word. The Greek word is *pistis* and is derived from *peitho*, which means "persuade, to be persuaded."[1] Once again, finding the etymology of a word is critical for us to understand the complete meaning.

The word *faith* actually means *persuasion*. Paul says that even our measure of faith comes from God. "Think of yourself with sober judgment, in accordance with the faith God has distributed to each of you" (Romans 12:3). Swapping out the word *persuasion* for *faith*, we see that God distributes to us a measure of persuasion. More importantly, God is doing His best to persuade the world into belief, never stopping or resting from this. That is why He sent His Son to overcome death. He was the only man to die and come back to life. This should be persuasion enough to believe; however, it doesn't always work that way. Even Thomas, one of the disciples, needed to touch the holes in Jesus's side and hands before he could be persuaded. To believe in our Lord Jesus is to have been persuaded into belief.

In the Bible, persuasion refers to the act of influencing. It involves presenting compelling arguments and evidence to bring about a change of heart or mind. The Greek word *peitho* signifies not only convincing someone through reasoning but also appealing to their emotions and moral character. The apostle Paul demonstrates the power of persuasion as he stands before King Agrippa. He says, "Do you believe the prophets? I know you do" (Acts 26:27). Paul skillfully engages Agrippa's familiarity with the Hebrew prophets, appealing to his knowledge and understanding. This form of persuasion seeks to connect with a recipient's existing beliefs and values to lead them toward a new perspective or decision.

Another biblical example of persuasion can be found in Paul's second letter to the Corinthians. Paul states, "Since, then, we know what it is to fear the Lord, we try to persuade others" (2 Corinthians 5:11). This example uses emotional appeal as a means of persuasion. It involves understanding the values, beliefs, and motivations of the audience, enabling the persuader to effectively communicate and bring about a change of heart. It is a powerful tool that, when employed with wisdom and integrity, can lead individuals to embrace new beliefs, adopt positive attitudes, and make transformative decisions in their lives.

The idea behind faith or persuasion is initiated by God. We are the responders. One might consider it to be the faith of God, not us. There is no boasting as to how much faith you carry because it all comes from God. "The righteous will live by faith" (Romans 1:17). The idea of persuasion helps me as I deal with the world of unbelievers. I know that God is at work persuading them, and with my presence and interaction with people, I may be a part of His persuasion. Paul writes, "Faith comes from hearing the message, and the message is heard through the word about Christ" (Romans 10:17). The words of the Bible are persuading our thoughts as believers and persuading those who don't yet believe. For the rest of this life as we know it, God will continue to persuade us, along with the entire world. That is a glorious fact!

The appearance of the word *faith* is made known with the arrival of Jesus. There are only two instances where faith is mentioned in the Old Testament, referring to trust in God. In the Old Testament, God spoke to His people through prophets. Jesus coming into the world is God speaking to us face-to-face. God's persuasion is pronounced by the interaction Jesus had directly with the people. We see this persuasion in Jesus's interaction with the apostles. God's persuasion is never ceasing for the believer in Christ, the indwelling of the Holy Spirit. Paul says,

> Now to him who is able to strengthen you according to my gospel and the preaching of Jesus Christ, according to the revelation of the mystery that was kept secret for long ages but has now been disclosed and through the prophetic writings has been made known to all nations, according to the command of the eternal God, to bring about the obedience of faith—to the only wise God be glory forevermore through Jesus Christ! Amen. (Romans 16:25–27 ESV)

OBEDIENCE MAKES ME HEAR

Obedience is a word used in Christianity, and often in a not-so-positive way. Throughout my life, I have been bludgeoned by this word. If my behavior was not fulfilling the expectations of another Christian, I was told I was being disobedient. Many pastors use the words *obedience* and *disobedience* to influence behavior within the congregation. The word *obedient* as defined by Webster's dictionary means "submissive to the restraint or command of authority: willing to obey."[2] I am not wired this way. The word reminds me of a trained dog that has gone to obedience training and has learned to stay within the confines of the commands. In my life, punishment has always been associated with being disobedient. I have heard, "God is punishing you for your disobedience."

The Greek word *hupakoé* that is translated *obedience* means, "the ability to hear, discern, or perceive." The word *hupakoé*, comes from the words *akoúō*, which means "to hear" and *hypo* which means "under, such as under authority."[3] To me, it means that God's wisdom is being conveyed by hearing and perceiving. The Bible speaks to us in the words of God, and we perceive its immense value.

God gave us free will, which is an amazing gift. We now compare God's persuasion to our own thinking. We have the free will to choose the wiser—our thinking or God's. God's wisdom in our life is an amazing gift. And even greater than that is His grace, which is always loving, always patient, always kind, and generous. "Love is patient, love is kind. It does not envy, it does not boast, it is not proud . . . Love never fails" (1 Corinthians 13:4, 8).

God is always persuading. He uses grace, love, and wisdom. Love never fails, and neither does God. Your life revolves around understanding who God is and how you are connected to Him. We are connected through His persuasion and our ability to comprehend this loving persuasion.

As we combine the understanding of persuasion (faith) and hearing (obedience), we start to see the pieces fall together, and it starts to make perfect sense. Now we understand that God is persuading us, through the Word and His Spirit, to listen to Him. God's Word speaks volumes, but many times we can hear the voice of the Spirit guiding us though our thoughts. That still, quiet, gentle voice harkens to us.

Hearing involves attentiveness and openness to listening to God's voice, whether through Scripture, prayer, or the promptings of the Holy Spirit. Hearing requires humility, quieting our own thoughts and desires to make space for God to speak to us so that we can allow His truth to penetrate our heart and mind. Submission is the natural response to listening. When we hear God's voice, His commands, and His teachings, we are called to respond.

Hearing God is of utmost importance because it aligns us with His thoughts, leads us to a life of fruitfulness, and fosters a deep and intimate relationship with our Creator. The Bible provides numerous insights into the significance of agreeing with God's commands and instructions.

First, agreeing with God demonstrates our love for Him. Our compliance is a tangible expression of our devotion to God, showing that we value His authority and trust His guidance. It is an act of surrender as we acknowledge He knows what is best.

Second, by reading the Word and spending time in prayer, we hear God who safeguards us from harm and leads us to a life of blessing. God's guidelines promote well-being and protect us from destructive consequences.

Additionally, hearing God strengthens our faith and deepens our relationship with Him. James encourages us,

> But be doers of the word, and not hearers only, deceiving yourselves. For if anyone is a hearer of the word and not a doer, he is like a man who looks intently at his natural face in a mirror. For he looks at himself and goes away and at once forgets what he was like. (James 1:22–24 ESV)

When we understand this, it opens the door for God to work in our lives, revealing His power, wisdom, and provision. Jesus says, "In the same way, let your light shine before others, that they may see your good deeds and glorify your Father in heaven" (Matthew 5:16). Our yielding to the will of God reflects the transformative power of God and can inspire others to seek Him.

Hearing flows from a heart that recognizes and submits to God's authority. It is not a reluctant or forced compliance but a willing surrender to God, and it is fueled by trust, knowing that God's ways are perfect. He desires what is best for us. Hearing involves aligning our actions, attitudes, and choices with His revealed truth.

Persuasion and hearing form a dynamic interplay in the life of a believer; however, I am still able to override this voice by free will. If I choose not to listen, whatever happens is the consequence of my own making. God guides us, directs us, and we make choices to listen or not.

God does not punish us, but circumstances do. Listening to God has its own reward, just as not listening brings its own consequences. Again, He does not punish us. He only encourages us with His infinite wisdom. God wants us to have rich lives that involve love and peace.

I was raised by my German grandmother who had raised four boys of her own. Her kindness and wisdom were overwhelming. When I would misbehave, she didn't spank. Her discipline came with words. "You are better than that," she would say. Those words would slay me, because I had so much respect for her, and she was right. When I knowingly sin, God accepts me with no condemnation, often accompanied by a voice saying, "You are better than that."

WORSHIP IS ACTION

Many of us have come to understand that the word *worship* means singing hymns and praises. The word *worship* is derived from an Old English word, *worthship*, which is a word that denotes the worthiness of the one receiving the special honor or devotion.[4] Over time, the meaning of *worthship* evolved to encompass reverence, adoration, and acts of devotion directed toward a higher power. In Greek, it also means to prostrate oneself, to bow down. It conveys a sense of reverence toward God.

Worship encompasses a heart posture of surrender, awe, and deep connection with the divine. It leads to adoration and recognizing God's greatness, majesty, and love. Through worship, believers seek to honor and glorify God, wanting to offer themselves to Him in response to His grace and mercy. After hearing His voice, we now come to the worship portion of our relationship with God. The word *worship* has its roots in the word *motion*.

The Greek word *proskuneó* means "to fall down/prostrate oneself to adore" or "the willingness to make all necessary physical gestures of obeisance."[5] In other words, it means to agree with God in thought and deed through action. The thing I find so amazing about God is that, even if I hear His voice but don't respond in action, He does not and will not give up on me. He will never stop persuading me—ever. Once again, it is God's grace and love that shines forth and never gives up on any of us. It is the constant voice of persuasion.

Worship is also used as an act of service. The Greek word *latreuó* means "to render religious service or homage, to worship."[6] Responding to God activates our service to Him. When we hear God's voice, one of the most appropriate and natural responses is to worship Him. Worship is an act of reverence, adoration, and surrender. Throughout the Bible, we see instances where individuals or communities encountered God's voice and responded with worship. "Come, let us bow down in worship, let us kneel before the LORD our Maker; for he is our God and we are the people of his pasture, the flock under his care" (Psalm 95:6–7).

Worship is an act of acknowledgment and implementation. When we hear God's voice, we are prompted to align our lives with His desire and purposes. "Yet a time is coming and has now come when the true worshipers will worship the Father in the Spirit and in truth, for they are the kind of worshipers the Father seeks. God is spirit, and his worshipers must worship in the Spirit and in truth" (John 4:23–24).

Worshiping God in response to hearing His voice fosters intimacy and deepens our relationship with Him. It is through worship that we encounter God's presence in a profound way, experiencing His peace, joy, and comfort. As we engage in worship, our hearts are opened to receive more of God's revelation and transformation. When we hear God's voice through His Word or personal revelation, worship is the fitting and correct response. It is the recognizing of His sovereignty, goodness, and faithfulness.

In putting all this together, God persuades us to listen, and when we follow through with what we have heard, our action is our worship. It honors God when we believe Him and when we act on what He has said. I love God and want to do what is pleasing to Him—not out of fear of punishment, but in all reverence of God. While hymns and songs are great ways to praise God, acting on His Word and Spirit is what I deem real worship.

Having these three words redefined has changed my life and understanding of God. I hope they will for you as well.

Reflection Questions

1. How have you defined faith? How would you define it now?

2. How has God directed you in hearing His word?

3. Describe a time you responded to what you heard, and knew you honored and worshiped God.

5

LAW AND THE FEAR
OF THE LORD

I believe the greatest lie that Satan deceived Eve with was, "You will be like God" (Genesis 3:5). That's exactly what happens to people who want to live by the law. They believe that if they follow all that the law requires, they will be like God. It is impossible for us to accomplish when even a stray thought can be a violation of the law.

Trying not to focus on something is the quickest way to find yourself focusing on it. Proverbs tells us that our thoughts direct our actions. "Keep your heart with all vigilance, for from it flow the springs of life" (Proverbs 4:23 ESV). The Ten Commandments, along with 613 other laws given for the Israelites to follow, are what Jesus came to free us from. He fulfilled all the requirements of the law (Matthew 5:17). Yet Christians live as if they are given the promise of freedom only to be tied to a set of laws that they have to maintain for their faith to be successful.

The first thing to consider about the Ten Commandments is that they are given by God as guidelines for daily living. That statement fits perfectly with the verse that speaks of our daily-bread living in Christ. Jesus ushers in the new covenant of grace and leads us in the spirit of forgiveness. Paul says, "For when we were in the realm of the flesh, the sinful passions aroused by the law [the Ten Commandments] were at work in us, so that we bore fruit for death" (Romans 7:5). Understand that God gave the Ten Commandments to the Hebrews to lead them, yet they aroused their sinful nature.

The law was to make the nation of Israel aware of their sinfulness and their rebellious nature toward God. The law was a measuring stick to be meditated upon to know how far short they fell from the goodness and purity of God's standard. The stone tablets of the law were carried in the Ark of the Covenant. The Ark was carried as a treasure chest, staying near to the hearts of the Hebrew nation. The law had no power to prevent sin, or to eternally save them. God created the system of sacrifice to show them His loving-kindness and His grace to forgive them. When a sin was committed in violation of the law, a sacrifice was made and the people asked for forgiveness so that they would be aware of God. His forgiveness pointed them toward Christ who would forgive and redeem them once and for all.

The nature of man is to rebel against God, which is the reason for the Fall of Adam and Eve and our inheriting their nature. That is also the history of the nation of Israel who He called a stiff-necked people in their rebellion and rejection of not only the Ten Commandments, but of God Himself. There was only one law in the time of Adam and Eve: do not partake of the fruit of one tree. They were to listen to God's authority to guide them, and they could not do it. They instead listened to an enticing, lawless, lying authority: Satan.

Why did God give us the law if He knew we could not fulfill it? The author of Galatians tells us: "Why, then, was the law given at all? It was added because of transgressions until the Seed to whom the promise referred had come. The law was given through angels and entrusted to a mediator" (Galatians 3:19). The law serves as a moral standard, revealing God's holy and righteous character. It highlights the divine standard of righteousness and exposes human sinfulness. "Yet if it had not been for the law, I would not have known sin. For I would not have known what it is to covet if the law had not said, 'You shall not covet'" (Romans 7:7 ESV).

Humans confuse what is right or wrong, so God spelled it out for them. "God's law was given so that all people could see how sinful they were. But as people sinned more and more, God's wonderful grace became more abundant. So just as sin ruled over all people and brought them to death, now God's wonderful grace rules instead, giving us right standing with God and resulting in eternal life through Jesus Christ our Lord" (Romans 5:20–21 NLT). He also gave us the law to serve as a guardian of human behavior: "So the law was our guardian until Christ came that we might be justified by faith" (Galatians 3:24).

In the old system of the law, a lawbreaker's guilt was used to remind him of God, and in response, he was to make a sacrifice. In our present standing, the Holy Spirit reminds us of our sin nature in grace, without condemnation. He leads us to praise God for our constant right standing before Him because of what was accomplished in Christ. Praising God in my sin changed me, not for the sin, but for His grace and forgiveness, regardless of the sin. It's very difficult to continue to sin while praising God, thinking of His love and acceptance.

We inherited the nature to rebel against God. God wrote the Ten Commandments knowing that we had this rebellious nature. The law becomes a temptation to do the opposite. If you do not believe we are born into this nature, just observe small children when they learn to say no and disobey parents and authority figures. God is the ultimate authority of our lives, and even with the indwelling Holy Spirit and our new nature, our old self still rebels and does not agree with God.

Living according to a standard of rules should lead us to exhaustion and spiritual weakness. That is the way we were created. We are supposed to surrender our pursuit of holiness to find rest in Him. Instead of focusing on what not to do, we are to focus on the grace that we received from Him. Grace goes hand in hand with unconditional love and peace. We shift our focus from rule-keeping to cultivating a vibrant relationship with God, falling in love with Christ. His grace empowers us to live according to His principles. Without confidence in the freedom God has given you, the more you will rely on the Law.

THE FEAR OF THE LORD

I have heard so many confusing thoughts around the fear of the Lord. You won't love or approach someone you are afraid of. I know this firsthand. My dad was a towering six feet five inches with a long, thunderous stride. He had his own childhood trauma and was an angry guy, and I was afraid of him. Because of that, I didn't have a single conversation with him until after my college graduation.

As a new Christian, I read about having a fear of the Lord. This fear of the Lord bothered me. Throughout the Old Testament, we can read about some devastating things God did, and because of that, people were afraid. Pastors would reinforce this fear of God in sermons and then try to smooth it over by stating the fear of God was respect. I have come to know it differently.

It was a *wow* moment for me when I discovered what the fear of the Lord was about. There is so much of the Bible that makes no sense if we don't receive understanding. I researched the fear of the Lord and found these verses from the Old Testament:

> "And he said to man, 'Behold, the fear of the Lord, that is wisdom, and to turn away from evil is understanding.'" (Job 28:28 ESV)

> "The fear of the LORD is hatred of evil. Pride and arrogance and the way of evil and perverted speech I hate." (Proverbs 8:13 ESV)

"The fear of the LORD is the beginning of wisdom; all those who practice it have a good understanding. His praise endures forever!" (Psalm 111:10 ESV)

"The fear of the LORD is the beginning of knowledge; fools despise wisdom and instruction." (Proverbs 1:7 ESV)

After reading commentaries and studying these verses, I have come to a simple conclusion: indeed, we are to respect God. More importantly, we are to agree with Him. That's what made King David a man after God's own heart. When God confronted David, he offered no excuses. He agreed with God. To me, agreeing with God is the definition of the fear of the Lord. It is not a fear that frightens me, but the fear encourages me to agree with God.

Reflection Questions

1. Do you find yourself trying to follow the law? Explain
    how you do or don't follow the law.
2. Why do you think God gave us the Ten
    Commandments?
3. What areas of your life could you surrender and agree
    with God right now?

6

REFLECTIONS OF LIGHT

In him was life, and that life was the light of
all mankind. The light shines in the darkness,
and the darkness has not overcome it.
– John 1:4–5

*I*n a world of darkness where people are separated from
God, light is a beautiful theme. God calls Himself
the light of men's lives. Light is a signal for guidance.
For decades, mariners navigated their vessels through the
waters of the unknown by the light of day and the lights
of the night in darkness. The most amazing scientific
aspect of light is that it travels invisibly through space
until it is reflected off something. All that is seen comes
from a source that is invisible. All that is illuminated is

a reflection from the source of light. Jesus is the light, the exact representation and reflection of God. He is "the true light that gives light to everyone was coming into the world. He was in the world, and though the world was made through him, the world did not recognize him" (John 1:9–10).

BELIEVERS AND APOSTLES

I want to include some overlooked reflections on subjects and ideas throughout the Bible so that you can enhance your thoughts on ways to view the meaning of the unseen thing. I take great liberty to view things outside the box of normal biblical interpretation. My purpose is to broker further understanding regarding our relationship with God and His Word. During my experience of walking with the Lord for forty years, I haven't seen many new understandings of the Bible. And yet it is a living Word, as alive as God is alive. Each time I read it, I receive some new understanding that springs forth to my thoughts, making it very alive. Below are some out-of-the-box reflections on subjects and ideas throughout the Bible to enhance your ways to viewing Scripture.

CONSTANTINE AND CHURCH HISTORY

The light of the Word was dimmed greatly during the reign of Constantine, the first Christian emperor of Rome.[1] From this period, we see great distortions entering the early Church. Constantine declared Christianity the state religion of Rome. From this time forward, pagan rituals became intermingled with the true Word of God. Many holidays and celebrations came from the pagans. The Greeks and Romans worshiped their gods Zeus, Apollo, and the like, who supposedly had supernatural powers. Mythology was incorporated into early Christian worship. It became popular to take this pagan worship and comingle it with Christianity. Christians began praying to and worshiping the apostles of the Bible and the Virgin Mary, crediting them with supernatural powers that come only from Christ. They also prayed to saints (exemplary Christians who had already died) who were in heaven and were thought to advocate things like a nation, place, craft, activity, or protection. Instead, all true power comes from the Almighty Father, the Son who was sent, and the Spirit who raised Christ from the dead. Amen.

The early Church was founded under Roman rule, and it eventually formed a God-government similar to Rome. The Church did not conquer Rome; Rome conquered the Church. The Vatican, which is its own country, is not the kingdom for which Christ died. The leadership of the early Church was divided with men assuming power over the Church of Christ. There is no evidence Peter declared himself pope, or with such authority as a pope. Instead, he admonished the leadership in the early Church:

> I appeal as a fellow elder and a witness of Christ's sufferings who also will share in the glory to be revealed: Be shepherds of God's flock that is under your care, watching over them—not because you must, but because you are willing, as God wants you to be; not pursuing dishonest gain, but eager to serve; not lording it over those entrusted to you, but being examples to the flock. And when the Chief Shepherd appears, you will receive the crown of glory that will never fade away. In the same way, you who are younger, submit yourselves to your elders. All of you, clothe yourselves with humility toward one another, because, "God opposes the proud but shows favor to the humble." (1 Peter 5:1–5)

The light grew dark with rituals, observances, and corruption around selling and granting absolution, which can only come from Jesus. These distortions grew with the lack of the written word. The printing press was not invented until the fifteenth century, which allowed leaders of the Church to distort God's Word. Without accountability, corruption ensued. "Power tends to corrupt and absolute power corrupts absolutely."[2] Many things were said of the Bible that are found nowhere in its contents.

The invention of the printing press had a profound impact on Christianity, bringing about significant changes that influenced the course of the religion's history. Before the printing press, the production of books—including Bibles—was a time-consuming and expensive process. With the advent of the printing press, the Bible could be mass-produced, making it more affordable and widely accessible to the general population. This led to an increase in biblical literacy and allowed individuals to study the Bible for themselves.

The era of the printing press paved the way for the Reformation. Reformers, such as Martin Luther, John Calvin, and others, utilized the printing press to disseminate their theological writings, pamphlets, and translations of the Bible. This facilitated the rapid spread of Reformation ideas, leading to religious reformation. People were able to read the Word of God for themselves, which made the way for Him to speak directly into their spirit.

As the abundance of Bibles accelerated around the world, the light kept getting brighter. Having been involved in Bible study for years, I would look at the commentaries of great theologians and find no new understanding of Scripture. This included the last five hundred years. I could clearly see a pattern of the theologians following the leaders of the early Reformation; however, these early reformers were faulty humans. They, too, had come from this era of darkness.

Much of what I have read in commentaries follows their thought processes. Few or no new considerations were added over time. I believe people are afraid to approach the Holy Scripture with fresh ideas for fear of ridicule and unacceptance. I for one have experienced this. People are still comforted and love their rituals and habits, thinking they win favor from God in what they do and don't do.

GRACE

The main truth hidden from both Christian believers and nonbelievers is the amazing grace of God. God is always persuading all people all the time. But what is He persuading us about? Only one thing: everything. First, He persuades us of His existence. Just look at the amazing aspects of nature and man. Have you noticed the complexity of His divine creation? When we are alone and in trouble, to whom can we cry out? Is there someone or something listening and responding? Of course there is! God calls to each of us with the voice of His persuasion.

I was blessed because my first pastor always said, "As you hear my preaching, never take my word for the things I say. Do research for yourself." That is exactly what I have done in these following pages. Many topics of the Bible and their explanations are difficult to understand. One of those is the topic of grace.

Grace, as understood in Christian theology, is the unmerited favor and loving-kindness of God extended to humanity. It is a concept deeply rooted in the Bible and carries significant meaning for believers. Webster's dictionary defines grace as "unmerited divine assistance given to humans for their regeneration or sanctification" and "a virtue coming from God."[3]

The Bible provides various verses that illuminate the nature of grace and its relationship to sin. The apostle Paul says "it is by grace you have been saved, through faith— and this is not from yourselves, it is the gift of God—not by works, so that no one can boast" (Ephesians 2:8–9). We see that salvation is a result of God's grace, not earned through human efforts. It is a gift freely given by God to those who believe in Him.

In another letter Paul affirms that transformative power of grace in relation to sin, stating that "sin shall no longer be your master, because you are not under the law, but under grace" (Romans 6:14). Grace empowers believers to resist sin and live in agreement with God. It is through the grace of God that believers are set free from the bondage of sin and are enabled to live in righteousness.

Webster's definition highlights that grace is divine assistance given for regeneration or sanctification. Regeneration refers to the spiritual rebirth and renewal that takes place when a person accepts Christ. Through God's grace, believers are transformed from a state of spiritual death and separation from God to a state of new life and restored relationship with Him.

This is but one example of confusion among believers. I believe love is understanding and being understood. I long for more understanding. We have a magnificent God who longs for our understanding and who longs that we fall more deeply in love with Him. Jesus has graced us with forgiveness and reconciliation to the Father. What greater sacrifice could be done than Him laying down His life for us? This was the greatest act of love in the history of mankind.

OUR RESPONSE

Our response should be to know Him better, to accept the gift of His unconditional love, and to align our thoughts with His thoughts. This should happen not because we have to, but because we want to "for the word of God is alive and active. Sharper than any double-edged sword, it penetrates even to dividing soul and spirit, joints and marrow; it judges the thoughts and attitudes of the heart" (Hebrews 4:12).

This is why I write. I am a layman and a believer. I am not a theologian who is guided by institutions. I have been guided by God in the understanding of His Word. I love God, and I want to know and understand Him. I want you to know and understand Him and to love Him. Falling in love with God—not being focused on what you do or don't do—is what brings about change in a person. Paul asked the Galatians, "Are you so foolish? After beginning by means of the Spirit, are you now trying to finish by means of the flesh?" (Galatians 3:3). He went on to chastising them for forgetting who they are in Christ:

> Formerly, when you did not know God, you were slaves to those who by nature are not gods. But now that you know God—or rather are known by God—how is it that you are turning back to those weak and miserable forces? Do you wish to be enslaved by them all over again? (Galatians 4:8-9)

The past has influenced the present of Christian belief with the assumption that the past has been correct in its understanding. As Christians, we all stand in Christ. With such a vast array of believers over history, we stand on ground they paved. For that, I am very grateful. The Lord could have not made it simpler: just accept the one true God, Jesus as God, and you are home. The Christian Church has embraced a method of evangelism that deals with having to feel badly about yourself, a horrible sinner, in order to know God. And if that is not bad enough, no good discussion is complete without the threat of death eternal. Instead, we should be persuading people to have faith in the loving living God.

God has not given up on mankind. In this period of grace, God is building His family. He calls Himself the God of Abraham, Isaac, and Jacob. This is the exact representation of family. Abraham the father, Isaac the son, and Jacob, those who are the sons of the son. This is the foreshadowing of God the Father, Jesus the Son, and with our belief in the Son, we become sons of the Son, "for in Christ Jesus you are all sons of God, through faith" (Galatians 3:26). We are all invited. He included the invitation to read, "The World." We are all children of God; however, not everyone calls Him Father. But He is constantly persuading us to come to Him. He wants a very personal relationship with us and is ready for an exchange—a life for a life, a death for a death.

Not only does God offer this great deal, but He comes after us to persuade us to trust in Him with our lives. As a Christian, I share in His persuasion from the day I claimed Him as my God. And my claim was so weak. All I said was, "Okay, Jesus. You are God." He immediately answered my understanding of Him and of His persuasion. God hooked me for a lifetime with His love.

So the point of all this persuasion from God is life everlasting. Our bodies are going to die. In the same way that God cast judgment on the earth in the days of Noah and all died (except Noah and his family), we will all die someday. God gave Noah the directions to build an ark. He persuaded Noah to do this, and Noah responded and was saved. God was showing Noah the way forward. The same is true of us now. The vision of God is forward moving. He is persuading us to see and understand His thoughts. Christ said He only did what He saw the Father doing (John 5:19). This could also be called persuasion. It was the same process that we go through, only Christ was more attuned and sensitive to the voice of the Father. Once you agree and think as God does, you will have gained His wisdom, and He gives you peace. This is the peace of God that surpasses your understanding (Philippians 4:7).

God's wisdom is the treasure of life. He is very patient with us regardless of how we disagree with Him or strive in our controlled, backward living, which most would call *sinfulness*. God does not see it that way. He is only and always showing you a way forward, not caring so much that you went backward, but helping you understand why you should want to move forward. To gain peace and wisdom by Him, in Him, and through Him.

Reflection Questions

1. Do you know God? How do you want to know more about Him?
2. Describe a time when you needed God's help in moving forward in your life.
3. Did you know about early church history? How is the church like a family?
4. Have you ever repressed your relationship with God? If so, why?

7

A HIDDEN TRUTH

There is so much truth in the Bible. In fact, all of it is true. How men interpret this truth is the question. The problem in many contemporary Christian churches in America is that we have become lazy and not attentive. Entertainment has become a main theme.

It is wise to exercise discernment and caution when it comes to believing everyone who stands in the pulpit or claims to teach God's Word. The Bible itself warns against false teachers and emphasizes the importance of testing the spirits to ensure their alignment with God's truth. Oftentimes, we are too willing to believe anyone who is in the pulpit, who has graduated from seminary, or who wears a fancy robe to prove their authority with God.

It is important for congregations to test the teachings that emanate from the pulpit to ensure that the messages align with the core principles of the faith. Moreover, testing the teaching encourages a deeper engagement with religious concepts and fosters a spirit of intellectual inquiry among believers. It promotes a healthy dialogue where Christians can openly discuss interpretations, ask challenging questions, and seek clarification on matters of doctrine and morality. This process not only strengthens the understanding of religious teachings but also guards against the potential misuse of authority or misinterpretation that could lead to division within the community.

As I participated in an international Bible study, I read in the weekly notes the following statement: The most important thing in a person's life is to have their sins forgiven. This sounds like good Christian theology; however, I was outraged. Is this really the most important thing in a person's life? What about being reconciled to God and having a relationship with Him? Jesus took care of the sin issue when He took away the sin of the world. We had nothing to do with it. He did it for us so that we could be reconciled to the Father. In this study, I was the only person outraged, which showed me how passive and vulnerable believers have become.

In John's letter, he advises the believers not to "believe every spirit, but test the spirits to see whether they are from God, because many false prophets have gone out into the world" (1 John 4:1). This verse highlights the need for discernment and careful evaluation of those who claim to speak on behalf of God. Not everyone who proclaims to be a teacher of the Bible may accurately represent its teachings or have genuine motives.

Messages that contain more milk than meat, and services where people are singing praises to God without knowing His true nature are filled with mixed and confused messages. With that in mind, I take to task many of the present teachings of the modern Christian Church. God bless the pastors and those who serve the Church and each other; however, I have run into well-intended teachings that have had horrible outcomes.

Jesus warns us to "watch out for false prophets. They come to you in sheep's clothing, but inwardly are ferocious wolves" (Matthew 7:15). This vivid metaphor underscores the importance of examining the character, teachings, and fruits of those who claim spiritual authority. There are those who may appear harmless or even righteous but who harbor misguided teachings that lead believers astray.

Jesus's teachings emphasize the fruits of these individuals, encouraging His followers to judge them by their actions and teachings rather than their outward appearance or charisma. He tells us that we "will recognize them by their fruits. Are grapes gathered from thorn bushes, or figs from thistles? So, every healthy tree bears good fruit, but the diseased tree bears bad fruit" (Matthew 7:16–17 ESV). This criterion of discernment emphasizes the practical outcomes and moral character produced by these individuals, urging His listeners to be vigilant in distinguishing truth from falsehood.

To avoid being led astray, I encourage you to develop a solid foundation in the Word of God. By immersing yourself in the Bible, cultivating a personal relationship with God, and being open to the guidance of the Holy Spirit, you can grow in discernment and recognize when teachings align with biblical truth or deviate from it. We must be committed to using discernment when we listen to a sermon or take someone else's interpretation of Scripture. As one of my first pastors said repeatedly, we were to listen to what he taught and then run it through our knowledge of Scripture before assimilating it into our theology.

Misinterpretations can arise from a failure to employ sound hermeneutical principles. Hermeneutics refers to the principles and methods used to interpret the Bible accurately. Neglecting to consider literary genres, historical context, the overall biblical narrative, and the original language can result in misinterpretations. It is vital to employ proper hermeneutical tools and seek guidance from trusted teachers, scholars, and commentaries to help navigate the complexities of scriptural interpretation.

Scripture interpretation requires careful study and an awareness of various factors that can influence our understanding. When interpretations are inaccurate, they can lead to misunderstanding, misapplication, and the distortion of God's intended message. One common issue in interpreting Scripture inaccurately is the failure to consider the historical and cultural context in which the biblical texts were written. The Bible was composed in specific time periods, cultures, and languages, and understanding the context is crucial for grasping the original meaning. Ignoring or misinterpreting the cultural norms, linguistic nuances, and historical circumstances can lead to misinterpretations that deviate from the intended message.

Another challenge is the tendency to read Scripture through personal biases or preconceived notions. When we approach the Bible with preexisting beliefs or agendas, we may inadvertently project our own ideas into the text, thus distorting its meaning. It is essential to approach Scripture with an open mind, humility, and willingness to be corrected by God's Word rather than using it to confirm our preconceived beliefs.

Ultimately, the problem of interpreting Scripture inaccurately highlights the need for humility. It is essential to approach Scripture with reverence, seeking the guidance of the Holy Spirit, and relying on the collective wisdom of the Christian community throughout history. By pursuing accurate interpretation, we can better grasp God's intended message and apply it faithfully to our lives for the glory of God and the edification of His people.

It is infrequent that we will ever find a church or pastor we totally agree with. It does not mean we should abandon or be in total disregard based on differences.

Questions to Reflect Upon

1.   How do you source your truth?

2.   Have you ever listened to and trusted the wrong person?
     What was the result?

3.   How can you be more discerning about what is being
      taught? Is there a time you did not agree with what was
      being taught? How did you respond?

8

THE LORD'S PRAYER

*S*o much of Scripture, the richness and meaning, is lost in the interpretation of others. With all the access we now have to study guides, online commentaries, and videos of people preaching, there is no reason not to study the Bible for ourselves.

I was reluctant to use a computer because I wasn't raised on one. Since I ventured into the cyberworld, I have found a vast amount of biblical knowledge. I can find the etymology and translations of words. With a simple understanding, I began looking up words in the original Greek and Hebrew languages. I came to a startling revelation around the Lord's Prayer:

> "Our Father in heaven, hallowed be your name. Your kingdom come, your will be done, on earth as it is in heaven. Give us this

day our daily bread, and forgive us our debts,
as we also have forgiven our debtors. And
lead us not into temptation, but deliver us
from evil." (Matthew 6:9–13 ESV)

While in my Bible study of the book of Matthew,
I became stuck. I knew that the Lord's Prayer could be
used as a pattern of prayer in any situation, but part of it
made no sense to me. Specifically, the verse I could not
settle was "Give us this day our daily bread" (Matthew
6:11). The Lord would not let me rest until I had a
better understanding of what that phrase meant. Most
of the commentaries I read said that this verse deals with
provision from the Lord. I could not accept this because
it does not fit with the rest of the prayer. Yes, the Lord
does give us provision—I am not arguing that point. All
that is given to me is from Him. I believe this verse opens
a window to the true meaning of the prayer.

Let's start by dissecting the prayer to discover the
meaning. In the context of the prayer, the first and
most important thing to consider is the audience. The
audience was the Hebrew people and possibly Gentiles.
The Hebrews had lost their faith in God throughout
the history of the Old Testament. Their loss of faith and
turning to other gods was disappointing to God. They
adopted the pagan ways and rituals of the foreigners
through idol worship. This was the main reason God

allowed the Babylonians to conquer the Hebrew nation. He had demonstrated to them His awesome power to rescue them, and the Hebrews still turned to other gods. He reached out with fellowship to them, and they did not respond.

FAITH

The connection between faith, the Hebrew people, and the Lord's Prayer is rooted in the shared spiritual heritage and the fundamental principles of trust and dependence on God. The Hebrew people experienced God's faithfulness, provision, and guidance throughout their history. The Lord's Prayer reflects the essence of faith and echoes the faith-filled journey of the Hebrew people.

Faith is at the core of both the Hebrew people's relationship with God and the Lord's Prayer. "Without faith it is impossible to please God, because anyone who comes to him must believe that he exists and that he rewards those who earnestly seek him" (Hebrews 11:6). The Lord's Prayer invites believers to align their hearts with the faith of the Hebrew people.

I submit that it was not so much the sinfulness of man that displeased God, but instead it was always about whether or not they had faith in Him. Faith is the main theme of the Bible. The faith of Noah saved mankind and all human existence. This was God's first act of salvation. By faith, Abraham was justified, declared righteous by God, and became the father of the Hebrew nation. King David, one of the most sinful characters of the Bible, a man after His own heart. Faith is always paramount in Scripture.

The Hebrew nation had again lost its true faith in God and its right standing before Him. The works and observance of their traditions had taken the priority over loving God. They believed their self-righteous behavior made them in good standing with God—not so different from today.

The Hebrew nation at the time of Christ was in disarray, with conflicts rising among the followers. There was a split in the nation between the Sadducees and the Pharisees. They believed the reason God allowed them to be conquered by the Babylonians was their disregard for the Hebrew law. This wasn't in any way the reason that God allowed this conquering. They had intermarried and lost the love of their one, true God. They had started worshiping the pagan gods of other tribes. With this fear that they hadn't followed the law fully, they added more rules, so they could be more specific about what was required of them.

Their good works—following the commandments and the religious rituals—were overriding faith and the love of God. This kind of belief system focused on their behavior and the behavior of others rather than on God. This is the audience Christ is speaking to with the Lord's Prayer.

Now that we understand that the audience was self-righteous believers, let's look at what God said through His prophet Jeremiah:

> "The days are coming," declares the LORD, "when I will make a new covenant with the people of Israel and with the people of Judah. It will not be like the covenant I made with their ancestors when I took them by the hand to lead them out of Egypt, because they broke my covenant, though I was a husband to them," declares the LORD. "This is the covenant I will make with the people of Israel after that time," declares the LORD. "I will put my law in their minds and write it on their hearts. I will be their God, and they will be my people. No longer will they teach their neighbor, or say to one another, 'Know the LORD,' because they will all know me, from the least of them to the greatest," declares the LORD. "For I will forgive their wickedness and will remember their sins no more." (Jeremiah 31:31–34)

The age to which Jeremiah is referring came when Christ appeared; He ushered it in. John the Baptist announced the arrival of the Anointed One. In those days, John the Baptist was preaching in the wilderness of Judea and saying, "Repent, for the kingdom of heaven has come near" (Matthew 3:2). I do not believe that the word *repent* used here means to repent of their sin. John is referring to their faith, as he is hoping to turn them from their works-oriented self-righteous belief systems back to faith and love of God.

The angel of God says this to Zacharias about the birth of John, and he will turn many of the children of Israel back to the Lord their God (Luke 1:16). Paul writes about how those who were zealous for God "did not know the righteousness of God and sought to establish their own, they did not submit to God's righteousness" (Romans 10:3). Faith is the only place where the righteousness of man prevails through God.

Man will always sin. All men have sinned since the time of the Fall. God gives a word through Jeremiah that one day He "will forgive their wickedness and will remember their sins no more" (Jeremiah 31:34)—only through faith in God. This is the new covenant, the kingdom to come through Christ the Lord. Without a doubt, the salvation of man and his restoration back to God was the single most important event in all human history. Keep in mind that at the time Jeremiah was prophesying, the crucifixion and resurrection of Christ had not yet come, so salvation and restoration had not yet happened.

THE PRAYER

The Lord's Prayer is filled with meaning, direction, and devotion. It reflects our longing for personal transformation as we acknowledge our need for sanctification and purification. We acknowledge that God's holiness should permeate every aspect of our lives. It is a prayer that our lives would bring honor and glory to God's name.

Our Father

"Our Father in heaven, hallowed be your name" (Matthew 6:9). This statement carries deep meaning and serves as a declaration of the sanctity of God. This is God, the Maker of heaven and earth, we are addressing. God is holy and is dwelling in the sanctified heavens. "Our Father" acknowledges the intimate and personal relationship that believers have with God through Jesus Christ. At the time Christ says this to the audience, it was considered blasphemy to reference God as Father, which was a reason they sought to kill Him.

The Hebrew nation of Israel was considered to be the children of God. It signifies our adoption as individual children of God and our privilege to approach Him with familiarity, trust, and dependency. It reflects the loving and compassionate nature of God as a Father who cares for His children, listens to their prayers, and provides for their needs.

"Hallowed be thy name" expresses a profound reverence for the holiness and greatness of God's name. *Hallowed* means "to sanctify" or "set apart as holy." In this phrase, we are acknowledging and honoring the sacredness of God's name. It emphasizes the awe and respect we should have toward God's character, His authority, and His divine nature.

By praying "Our Father, hallowed be thy name," we are surrendering ourselves to God, aligning our hearts with His as the one with authority over all. It is an act of submission, recognizing that God's name and His kingdom are of utmost importance. We acknowledge that God's name is above all other names.

Your Kingdom Come

"Your kingdom come, your will be done, on earth as it is in heaven" (Matthew 6:10). This phrase expresses a heartfelt longing and surrender to the reign and rule of

God. It is a plea for the establishment and expansion of God's kingdom in our lives and the world around us.

When we pray, "Your kingdom come," we acknowledge God's sovereignty and His divine authority over all creation. It is an expression of our desire to see His righteous and loving rule manifested in every aspect of life. We recognize that God's kingdom operates on principles of justice, mercy, forgiveness, love, and righteousness. By praying for His kingdom to come, we are asking for God to take the throne of our life. We are no longer in control, trusting the lordship of God.

This phrase also carries an eschatological dimension, pointing toward the future consummation of God's kingdom at the end of time. It anticipates the fulfillment of God's promises, the defeat of evil, and the establishment of a new heaven and earth under His reign. In this sense, it is a longing for the ultimate restoration and redemption of all things, where God's perfect kingdom is fully realized.

Christ repeatedly said that we were to repent because the kingdom of heaven was near. God's kingdom is mentioned over thirty-four times in Matthew, and Jesus announces and enables the ushering in of the kingdom. The will of God is that all men should have salvation and be joined with Him forever. Heaven is the dwelling place of God and eternal life, which is offered to all men and women on earth. It is the kingdom of God within you. Heaven and earth joined in eternal life through the Savior. In addition, through Christ and the Spirit, man will be able to give up his desire to rebel against God. He will also have the desire, through the Spirit of God, to agree with Him in thought and deed.

When Jesus's disciples prayed "Your kingdom come" they were praying for a kingdom that had not yet arrived. The kingdom was among them in the Lord Jesus but not yet "in them." After the resurrection of Christ, He sent the Holy Spirit to live in us, and we became dwellers in God's kingdom, forever.

Your Will Be Done

This part of the prayer has a major significance. The kingdom of God will arrive by the will of God. A will, or a testament, is what is left behind after death. Fulfilling the will of God was Jesus's purpose. "'Sacrifices and offerings… you did not desire, nor were you pleased with them'—though they were offered in accordance with the law. Then he said, 'Here I am, I have come to do your will.' He sets aside the first to establish the second. And by that will, we have been made holy through the sacrifice of the body of Jesus Christ once for all" (Hebrews 10:8–10).

On Earth as it is in Heaven

It is the will of God that all people on earth should have salvation and live eternally with Him. He is gathering a family from earth through belief in His Son. It starts on earth and continues eternally in heaven. "He made known to us the mystery of his will according to his good pleasure, which he purposed in Christ, to be put into effect when the times reach their fulfillment—to bring unity to all things in heaven and on earth under Christ" (Ephesians 1:9–10).

Give Us This Day Our Daily Bread

"Give us this day our daily bread" (Matthew 6:11 ESV). This is the part of the prayer in which the Holy Spirit would not let me rest. It made no sense to me that the phrase could be addressing provisions related to the kingdom that is about to come. *Give us this day* means "a time of" or "an age of." Jeremiah said, "The days are coming" (Jeremiah 31:31). This day will contain daily bread.

Instead of thinking of bread as food or sustenance, I believe that it is none other than Christ Himself. Asking for daily bread can be understood as seeking spiritual nourishment from God and desiring His presence, love, wisdom, and guidance in our lives. It symbolizes that our hunger should be for a close relationship with the living God. Showbread is the "bread of the presence" of God in the Hebrew Temple. Jesus represents the bread of the presence of God with us.

> "I am the bread of life." (John 6:48)

> "For the bread of God is the bread that comes down from heaven and gives life to the world." (John 6:33)

> "I am the bread of life. Whoever comes to me will never go hungry and whoever believers in me will never be thirsty." (John 6:35)

He identifies Himself as the bread that truly satisfies and sustains our deepest spiritual hunger. Through His life, death, and resurrection, Jesus provides the nourishment and fulfillment our souls crave: "While they were eating, Jesus took bread, and when he had given thanks, he broke it and gave it to his disciples, saying, 'Take and eat; this is my body'" (Matthew 26:26).

We now understand that when Jesus said "Give us this day our daily bread," He was talking about the fact that He is the bread. This interpretation of the word *bread* makes sense. He is our daily sustenance for life everlasting. He is the ultimate source of true spiritual nourishment as seen in John 6:25–59, which is a beautiful dissertation of Jesus as the Bread of Life.

When we pray, "give us our daily bread," we are not solely asking for physical sustenance. We are acknowledging our dependence on Jesus, the bread of life, for our spiritual nourishment and well-being. We recognize that the bread—Jesus—is in us and is working through us.

Keep in mind that the mission of the Lord was not yet finished when He shared this prayer. He was to usher in the age of grace and forgiveness, which we see ties into the next verse.

And Forgive Us Our Debts

"And forgive us our debts, as we also have forgiven our debtors" (Matthew 6:12). This phrase holds significant spiritual and relational implications. It is an acknowledgment of our need for mercy and grace. Romans tells us that the wages of sin is death (Romans 6:23). There are debt wages to be paid to God for sin. And this is the forgiveness of that debt by the work of Christ on the cross. He paid the wages for us.

This prayer is addressed to God the Father to forgive this debt, the fulfillment of God's promise in Jeremiah. Once again, this prayer is focused on the mission of Christ to complete the promise of forgiveness by God. In so doing, the believer's gratefulness to Him and the Holy

Spirit enables us to forgive others their offenses against us (see Ephesians 4:32 and Colossians 3:13).

Lead Us Not Into Temptation

"And lead us not into temptation but deliver us from the evil one" (Matthew 6:13). What a difficult verse this is! It appears to fly in the face what James said: "When tempted, no one should say, 'God is tempting me.' For God cannot be tempted by evil, nor does he tempt anyone" (James 1:13).

Into implies the motion toward or penetration. Not into would be to move away from. This prayer is asking God to lead us away from temptations. When Christ completes His mission on the cross, we are left with the Holy Spirit to guide us away from temptations. "No temptation has overtaken you except what is common to mankind. And God is faithful; he will not let you be tempted beyond what you can bear. But when you are tempted, he will also provide a way out so that you can endure it" (1 Corinthians 10:13).

Deliver Us From Evil

The Spirit of God had departed from Adam and Eve because they believed the words of a different authority,

Satan, a liar and deceiver. They had partaken of the knowledge of evil. We see evil flourishing immediately when Cain killed his brother Abel (see Genesis 4). The knowledge of evil is what has killed mankind. Man has shown an inability to overcome this force.

The spiritual warfare on earth as it is in heaven is a battle for the loyalty of mankind. Who will we follow? Christ was very concerned about His disciples when He prayed for their protection before He departed this earthly realm: "I have given them your word and the world has hated them, for they are not of the world any more than I am of the world. My prayer is not that you take them out of the world but that you protect them from the evil one" (John 17:14–15).

Delivering us from the evil one is exactly what Christ has done for us. He "gave himself for our sins to rescue us from the present evil age, according to the will of our God and Father, to whom be glory forever and ever" (Galatians 1:4–5). This is very similar to the end of the Lord's Prayer, and not by coincidence. This shows the desire of the Father to restore us to Himself. "We know anyone born of God does not continue to sin; the one who was born of God keeps him safe, and the evil one cannot harm him" (1 John 5:18). Timothy tells us the Lord will rescue us "from every evil attack and will bring

[us] safely to his heavenly kingdom. To him be glory for ever and ever" (2 Timothy 4:18).

Christ was to deliver us from evil with a heart that is sealed with the Holy Spirit. Here is a great summation of how Christ is the fulfillment of this prayer:

> Therefore, brothers and sisters, since we have confidence to enter the Most Holy Place by the blood of Jesus, by a new and living way opened for us through the curtain, that is, his body, and since we have a great priest over the house of God, let us draw near to God with a sincere heart and with the full assurance that faith brings, having our hearts sprinkled to cleanse us from a guilty conscience and having our bodies washed with pure water. Let us hold unswervingly to the hope we profess, for he who promised is faithful. (Hebrews 10:19–23)

For Yours is the Kingdom

"For thine is the kingdom and the power and the glory forever. Amen" (Matthew 6:13 KJV). It is argued that this closing verse was added in later manuscripts. Even if it was, it does not matter because it is truth. It is His kingdom and power forever. Paul uses this very same phrase in Galatians 1:5 and in 2 Timothy 4:18. Those citations were quoted in the previous paragraph. How can we not agree it fits?

In summary, I fail to see how anyone cannot see that this prayer was prayed, asked, and answered. Once again, this was to be the single most important event in the history of all mankind. Christ is asking the audience to pray that He would fulfill this promise of God. He was asking them to pray for Jesus, the Bread of Life, to fulfill His mission on the cross, to give "himself up for us as a fragrant offering and sacrifice to God" (Ephesians 5:2) once and for all.

Jesus said, "Here I am, I have come to do your will" (Hebrews 10:9). He sets aside the first to establish the second. And by that will, we have been made holy through the sacrifice of the body of Jesus Christ once for all. Christ set aside the old covenant with Moses, the law and the sacrifices, to establish the new covenant, and He is the fulfillment of the promise of Jeremiah 31, a prayer answered by Christ when, as He died, said, "It is finished" (John 19:30).

Now, we can use the pattern of this prayer to formulate a new one in the Spirit of Christ. This is the way I write it, and my hope is that you will find a way to write it for yourself to share with others.

Our father who gathers us as family in heaven, with Christ seated at your right hand, hallowed be your name. Praise and glory be to you, oh, God, for your kingdom has come and your will is being done on earth as it is in heaven. Thank you for giving us this day and age of grace, and for you, Christ, our daily bread. Thank you for your forgiveness and redemption and with our gratefulness to you and in your Spirit of love and forgiveness we are able to forgive those who trespass against us. Thank you for no longer leading us by testing our heart by the law with sin and guilt but by writing the law in our hearts to agree with you and not rebel against you, by your Spirit. Thank you for rescuing us from evil for sanctifying us in Christ so that we spend eternity with you, no matter how many times we should trespass against you. We have been delivered from evil. Thank you, for yours truly is the kingdom, the power, and the glory of us and everything, all in all, forever and ever. Amen.

It is my hope that when you hear the Lord's Prayer, you can remember with confidence that what you are praying was asked and answered. I hope that the new revelation of this prayer will fill your heart with joy as it has mine. I pray that you will know the meaning and fulfillment of the statement "It is finished."

Reflection Questions

1. What did you learn about the Lord's Prayer?
2. What new insights might have changed some of your understanding about God through this knowledge?
3. Write your own Lord's Prayer based off what you learned.

9

GENESIS

The more I read the book of Genesis, the more I see the essence and character of both man and God. Many consider the book a fairy tale; however, we are children of God with limited knowledge of Him. To those who mature in God, this book contains so many deep answers that beg even more questions.

CREATION

The beginning is when God created things. We don't know when that was, and it is still a mystery of science. With great certainty, scientists understand how it was made. It was formed from something with infinite density that was heated to an infinite temperature. It exploded at infinite pressure. Everything we see in the heavens at night was originally formed from something no bigger than a pin head.[1] This is mind boggling.

Even more marvelous in all creation is that God gave life to man and woman, created them in His own image. We were created in God's image of pureness, goodness, and holiness. God named the first man Adam, which means red earth. The color red is symbolic of fire throughout the Bible. This is reflected today in how our fire departments use red for their trucks and logos. I believe Adam, who was formed from the dust of the earth, was given the red fire of the Holy Spirit. Man was created pure, without sin, and with free will.

A rebellion in heaven took place with a prideful and power-hungry angel named Lucifer. He thought himself to be as God, not created by God. The angel Lucifer, who was cast out from heaven and is now called Satan, still had dominion to visit God's creation, earth, and to influence man's thoughts toward pride and destruction. The name Satan means "to oppose," and that is his influence in our nature.[2] God's original, beautiful creation was influenced as Adam and Eve ate of the tree of the knowledge of good and evil. We were influenced to oppose or rebel against God. Our job is to agree with the mind of God.

The most important part of this story is that there was just one commandment or boundary in all of creation, the same as today. That directive was to believe God. To believe God is what redeemed Abraham, the first born of the Jews, back to relationship with God. To believe Jesus is God's only begotten son is what redeems us to an eternal existence with God. Nothing is different or has been changed from the very beginning of creation. God spoke to His creation and filled a garden with trees and animals and all kinds of beauty.

I believe many of the trees of the garden were special trees, yielding God's fruit of the Spirit to mankind. Fruit from a tree is something to be ingested and consumed. A burning bush contained the Spirit of God as He instructed Moses. I believe the fruit from the tree was like a library of new thoughts Adam and Eve downloaded. Today, scientists can trace thoughts with computer imaging, and as thoughts race through the mind, the traces of them appear as trees, sprouting numerous branches.

The thoughts of good and evil were included on a tree in the garden. Only God can contain the thoughts of good and evil and not sin or be tempted. Adam and Eve loved God as He walked with them in the garden. They knew only of His purity and His thoughts. Now the voice of Satan came to them enticing them with thoughts that they could be like God. Satan's pride—thinking he could be as God—was his downfall. There is a difference between being like God or being God.

To be like God was a good thing for Eve and Adam. They knew only of His love and purity from the beginning. The epitome of admiration is emulation. Have you ever met someone you extremely admired and wanted to be like them? Satan used this to lure Eve with her desire to be like God. He took something very good—that they loved and admired God—and turned it into something dangerous. Satan's voice was something new and different in the garden. Without having had any previous experience with the concept of deception, they were unaware that this voice meant them harm. With the innocence of a newborn baby, they had no reason to distrust.

THE FALL

Adam and Eve were placed in the garden of Eden, a paradise filled with abundant beauty and harmony where they enjoyed a close relationship with God and communion with nature. In this perfect environment, Adam and Eve lived in innocence and without shame, completely open before each other and before God.

Doubt

Satan introduced doubt to Adam and Eve. He wanted them to doubt what God had said to them regarding the forbidden tree. He introduced doubt to them by questioning and distorting God's words and intentions. In the form of a serpent, Satan approached Eve and engaged her in a conversation designed to undermine her trust and faith in God.

In Genesis 3:4–5, we see Satan contradicting God's warning about the consequences of eating from the forbidden tree, saying, "You will not certainly die…. For God knows that when you eat from it your eyes will be opened, and you will be like God, knowing good and evil." With these words, Satan sowed doubt and deceived Eve by portraying God as withholding something desirable from Adam and Eve. He falsely promised that they would gain superior knowledge and become like God. This deception played on their curiosity, fostering a false desire to be like God.

Once Eve stepped across the line of doubt, she became the prey of the destroyer, and the history of mankind changed forever. This doubt ultimately led to disobedience. Our inheritance became doubt, rebellion toward God, and the nature of Satan.

It is important to note that Satan's strategy in introducing doubt is often characterized by questioning God's truth, distorting His Word, and appealing to our curiosity. Through these tactics, he seeks to undermine our trust in God and to entice us to pursue our own desires rather than submitting to God.

Satan's tactics have never changed. He still entices mankind in the same way he seduced Eve, through the lust of the flesh, the pride of life, and the promise that we would not die—the same temptations Jesus faced (Matthew 4:1–11). He was asked to turn rocks to bread, which was the lust of the flesh. He was offered the many kingdoms of the earth, which was the pride of life. And casting Himself off the pinnacle and being protected by angels was the enticement that He would not die. Nothing has changed with the deceiver.

SHAME

Their disobedience to God's command led to the fear of God and a sense of shame, to the point that they hid from Him. For the first time in their lives, Adam and Eve believed there was something inadequate about themselves. They sensed something was wrong with their bodies, that they needed to be covered, so they used fig leaves.

Shame is a powerful emotion and can have a profound impact on human behavior. When we experience shame, particularly as a result of our actions or choices, it often leads to a natural inclination to justify our behavior. This response stems from a desire to protect oneself from the discomfort and vulnerability that shame brings. We see this when Adam stated, "The woman you put here with me—she gave me some fruit from the tree, and I ate it" (Genesis 3:12). Adam blames God for giving him the woman. He tries to shift the blame onto others instead of taking full responsibility for his disobedience.

Purity

The complete and total pureness of God and His Spirit in them departed. Before their disobedience, Adam and Eve enjoyed a perfect and intimate relationship with God, free from sin and its corrupting influence. Their hearts and minds were untainted, and they lived in perfect harmony with God and each other; however, when Adam and Eve ate from the forbidden tree, their innocence was replaced. No longer did they have pure thoughts regarding God and a relationship with Him or each other. They became focused on themselves. I believe the first act of this corrupted nature came in the form of sexual lust for one another. The word *naked* appears in Leviticus and refers to sexual relations. Compare the King James Version and the New International Version:

> "None of you shall approach to any that
> is near of kin to him, to uncover their

nakedness: I am the LORD. The nakedness of thy father, or the nakedness of thy mother, shalt thou not uncover: she is thy mother; thou shalt not uncover her nakedness." (Leviticus 18:6–7 KJV)

"No one is to approach any close relative to have sexual relations. I am the LORD. Do not dishonor your father by having sexual relations with your mother. She is your mother; do not have relations with her." (Leviticus 18:6–7 NIV)

I believe the first thought aroused after the Fall was lust. I believe lust, objectifying each other, and not love, was something new to them, resulting in their shame, hiding from God, and covering their genitals. What a profound effect this has had on mankind throughout the ages.

Sexual lust can be as addictive as any drug, with devastating consequences. Look at the string of consequences King David experienced as the result of his lust. The son of King David, Solomon, was also enticed by numerous wives and concubines who led him away from God. Even with all of Solomon's wisdom, he could not be protected from the sexual lust of his heart. So many pastors in our modern era have fallen prey to sexual immorality.

Sexual lust is named numerous times in the New Testament as the first of importance in the many sins we are to guard our heart against. I think God instituted circumcision as a sign in the seed covenant he made with Abraham because of this sexual lust of the flesh. I believe it was also used to remind them to separate their lust of the flesh from God.

The loss of innocence resulted in several profound effects. First, it brought a separation between humanity and God. The pureness and holiness required to dwell in God's presence were compromised by sin. The loss of pureness severed the intimate communion they once had with their Creator.

Also, the Fall introduced a corrupted nature into the human condition. The purity of heart and mind that Adam and Eve possessed was tainted by the knowledge of good and evil. Sin distorted their perceptions, desires, and motivations. The purity of their intentions and actions was now marred by self-interest, pride, and disobedience.

The consequence of this loss of pureness extended beyond Adam and Eve. This is the condition in which mankind finds himself. We do not focus on God. Instead, we focus on what is good or evil and measure ourselves against it.

Not Abandoned

God did not abandon them. He pursued them in the garden. He sought them out and comforted them in their shame. He provided an animal to cover their shame of sin and guilt, foreshadowing the sacrificial system and pointing toward the ultimate sacrifice of Jesus Christ to remove our sins and restore our relationship with God.

God never broke relationship with Adam and Eve, as some would teach. He continued to pursue a relationship with them. God has never given up on us. He has always wanted a relationship with us in spite of our good or evil actions and thoughts. Through Christ, we find forgiveness, redemption, and liberation from the shame of our sin.

Before all this happened God told them they would die or cease to exist if they did not believe Him. This rings true throughout all mankind's existence. All have died from this point on. The attrition due to death is 100 percent, as God is true to His word. God did not allow them, or us, to live forever with a sin nature attached. We die as the result of not believing in God through faith. We are still hiding from God. We are God's children. He loves us and has provided the path of redemption by just one thing and one thing only: faith in Him. He is so good and loving toward us. Always and forever, the God I know.

PICTORIALS

Hebrew pictorials, also known as Paleo-Hebrew pictographic script, are a method of interpreting and understanding Hebrew words by examining their ancient pictorial origins. The Hebrew language, particularly in its earlier forms, was written using a system of characters that were originally derived from pictographic representations of objects, actions, or concepts. Each Hebrew letter had a corresponding pictorial meaning, and when combined, these letters formed words that carried both phonetic and visual significance. By understanding the pictorial meanings of the Hebrew letters, one can gain deeper insights into the underlying concepts and symbolism of Hebrew words.

The ancient translations of Hebrew pictorials are a lost language. The pictorials were abandoned in the Hebrew language, and when Arabic was incorporated into Hebrew script as the Babylonians conquered Israel, some of the true meanings of the words were lost. Scholars have done their best with what is available. It is important to note that Hebrew pictorials are not the sole means of interpreting Hebrew words, and their usage requires careful study and expertise.

When I look at the roots of words from the Genesis account, I have discovered some meanings associated with the Fall of man and the curse placed on Adam. The modern translation says that God cursed the ground.

THE CURSE

After Adam and Eve disobeyed God's command in the garden of Eden, their sin brought consequences not only to themselves but to mankind. One of the significant outcomes of their disobedience was the curse that fell upon the ground. God pronounces the consequences: "To Adam he said, 'Because you listened to your wife and ate fruit from the tree about which I commanded you, "You must not eat from it," 'Cursed is the ground because of you; through painful toil you will eat food from it all the days of your life. It will produce thorns and thistles for you and you will eat the plants of the field'" (Genesis 3:17–18).

The etymology of the word *ground* unlocks understanding of the curse. *Ground* has the root meaning in Adam not the earth.[3] In fact, Adam means red earth.[4] Adam was formed out of the dust of the earth, and as I stated previously, I believe that the "ruddy" aspect of Adam is the Holy Spirit. The Holy Spirit is referred to as a fire, and, of course, fires are red. Hence, Adam is the man formed from the dust of the earth with fire. The curse of the ground is the curse on all mankind.

These verses paint a picture of what will happen as the result of consuming the knowledge of good and evil. Thorns and thistles become the sting of death. The apostle Paul writes of this: "The sting of death is sin, and the power of sin is the law. But thanks be to God! He gives us the victory through our Lord Jesus Christ" (1 Corinthians 15:56–57).

Adam and Eve broke the only law, and now death arrives to mankind. Thorns and thistles will grow. As more knowledge of evil is consumed, evil will grow all the more. Mankind becomes so consumed with evil that they can't see the redeeming qualities of God—except in the family of Noah before the Flood.

Jesus also described the ground as mankind in the parable of the seed and the sower:

> "Listen! A farmer went out to sow his seed. As he was scattering the seed, some fell along the path, and the birds came and ate it up. Some fell on rocky places, where it did not have much soil. It sprang up quickly, because the soil was shallow. But when the sun came up, the plants were scorched, and they withered because they had no root. Other seeds fell among thorns, which grew up and choked the plants, so that they did not bear grain. Still other seed fell on good soil. It came up, grew and produced a crop, some, multiplying thirty, some sixty, some a hundred times.

Then Jesus said, 'Whoever has ears to hear,
let them hear.'" (Mark 4:3–9)

Some seed fell among the thorns, which represents
the temptations of the world and sin. The thorns or
temptations choked out the Word of God, just as in the
garden of Eden. The curse of the thorns and thistles,
which is sin and death, appears again with Abraham when
he offered his son as a sacrifice to God. In what I believe
is one of the most moving stories in the Bible, Abraham's
love for God is tested. God requires Abraham to sacrifice
his son to cover his sin. As Abraham complies and raises
his hand to sacrifice Isaac, God holds back His hand.
Instead, God provides the sin offering, a ram that has
his head caught in a thicket. I believe this to symbolize a
crown of thorns and thistles, which is foreshadowing the
crown of thorns placed on Christ on the way to the cross.
God stays the sacrifice of the miraculously born Isaac, the
only son of Abraham.

It appears to me that God is telling Abraham that it
won't be Abraham's son but God's Son who will be the
ultimate sacrifice. The love of God is on display. God
will create the immaculate conception of Christ, the only
Son of God, and sacrifice Christ as a sin offering for the
world. Before hanging on the cross, Jesus had a crown of
thorns and thistles forced onto his head. He was crowned
with the curse of mankind, sin and death.

We see thorns in Paul's letter to the Corinthians. He describes having a thorn in his flesh:

> In order to keep me from becoming conceited, I was given a thorn in my flesh, a messenger of Satan, to torment me. Three times I pleaded with the Lord to take it away from me. But he said to me, "My grace is sufficient for you, for my power is made perfect in weakness." Therefore I will boast all the more gladly about my weaknesses, so that Christ's power may rest on me. That is why, for Christ's sake, I delight in weaknesses, in insults, in hardships, in persecutions, difficulties. For when I am weak, then I am strong. (2 Corinthians 12:7–10)

I believe this thorn in the flesh given to Paul was some type of sin he was dealing with. That's why he writes of God's grace being sufficient for him. The most encouraging words for all of us who sin and fall short: "For when I am weak, then I am strong." The strength to overpower sin is not in us; it's in God. That's why Paul is strong. Jesus won the victory of sin for us on the cross.

BROTHER KILLS BROTHER

Look at the first generation from Adam and Eve. A brother kills a brother (Genesis 4:1–16). Why? Jealousy. One brother loved God more than the other, which is demonstrated through his offering made to God. This rejection caused Cain to become jealous and resentful toward his brother. In his anger, Cain lured Abel into a field and killed him out of jealousy.

Jealousy came from Satan. The tragic event of Cain killing Abel is a stark illustration of the destructive power of jealousy and its consequences. It reveals the destructive nature of sin and its ability to lead to extreme actions. Cain's jealousy blinded him to reason, love, and the value of human life. This story serves as a warning about the destructive potential that jealousy has.

From generation to generation in the book of Genesis, we see the hardening of hearts toward God. This hardening of hearts refers to a gradual turning away from God's ways, a stubborn resistance to His guidance, and an increasing inclination toward sin and rebellion. In the Old Testament, we witness numerous instances where successive generations failed to heed God's commands and chose to follow their own desires instead. In the book of Judges, for example, after Joshua and the generation that experienced the miraculous deliverance from Egypt and entrance into the promised land, a cycle of disobedience, oppression, repentance, and deliverance emerged. Each successive generation seemed to drift further from God's ways and became prone to idolatry and rebellion.

This resulted in the total abandonment of man from God.

NOAH AND HIS FAMILY

The only exception is Noah and his family. "Noah was a righteous man, blameless among the people of his time, and he walked faithfully with God" (Genesis 6:9). During Noah's time, humanity had become exceedingly wicked and corrupt. "The LORD regretted that he had made human beings on the earth, and his heart was deeply troubled" (Genesis 6:6). The Lord was grieved He had made man on the earth, and His heart was filled with pain.

Noah, however, found favor in the eyes of God due to his righteousness and faithfulness. He walked with God, meaning he listened to and worshiped God, and he sought to please Him in all aspects of his life. Because of Noah's righteousness, God chose him to build an ark and be the instrument of salvation for his family and representatives of all living creatures. Noah faithfully followed God's instructions and, along with his wife, three sons, and their wives, entered the ark before the great flood came upon the earth.

Noah's righteousness is further emphasized by the fact that he was the only one in his generation to find favor with God. His obedience and trust in God's promises resulted in his family being saved from the destruction that befell the rest of humanity.

THE FLOOD

God's first act of salvation is in Genesis with the story of Noah and the Flood. Almost all religions have a flood account. People throughout the world have the same story that has been handed down from generation to generation about water covering the earth. We know from the Bible what the Flood did. It destroyed every evil human and allowed the world to start new and fresh with people of faith. Noah, a righteous man, saved the earth and everything that breathed. The earth was cleansed during the flood as evil was done away with... albeit temporarily.

Noah, in a sense, is the forerunner of Jesus, having saved the world through his faith and belief in God. Please notice that the Bible does not say he was blameless before God; instead, it says he was blameless among the people of his time. No one born of Eve is ever blameless before God. The violence on the earth was so great that God set out to destroy all mankind but allowed Noah and his family to be saved. The ark becomes the ark of salvation for Noah and his family, being sealed in it by God Himself. It passed through the waters of God's judgment to keep Noah and his family alive.

This is so important to the understanding of baptism as we know it. Peter describes baptism in this very same way:

> God waited patiently in the days of Noah while the ark was being built. In it only a few people, eight in all, were saved through water, and this water symbolizes baptism that now saves you also—not the removal of dirt from the body but the pledge of a clear conscience toward God. It saves you by the resurrection of Jesus Christ, who has gone into heaven and is at God's right hand—with angels, authorities and powers in submission to him. (1 Peter 3:20–22)

After forty days on the ark, Noah sent out a dove three times to see if the waters had receded. The first time the dove came back after flying and not having a place to land. After waiting seven days, the dove was sent out again and returned in the evening with an olive branch. That demonstrated to Noah that the water had receded. The third time the dove was sent forth, it did not return to the ark of salvation Noah had built.

THE DOVE

The Holy Spirit descended on Jesus in the form of a dove. Many wonder why Jesus sought John the Baptist and why He chose to be baptized. The answer is in 1 Peter. It is His public appearance before man to show and proclaim His faith in God. This is why John was baptizing men into faith. It was the fulfillment or completion of all righteousness as Jesus states, "Let it be so now; it is proper for us to do this to fulfill all righteousness" (Matthew 3:15).

The completion of righteousness comes through faith and faith alone. The righteousness that comes by faith is the declaration of Jesus to John and the world.

As a Christian walking with the Lord for forty-four years, I never heard or read that baptism had been around two hundred years or so prior to John. It was the last ceremonial cleansing in a ritual that brought Gentiles into belief in Judaism. Notice I say belief in Judaism rather than belief or faith in God. The Jews of Jesus's time had become comfortable with the traditions of their religion and basically abandoned faith in God. That's why so many times they wanted to kill Jesus even though the Ten Commandments told them that they should not kill. He violated their rituals. If a Jew obeyed and observed the rituals, he was in good standing with the religious leaders. That did not include good standing before God.

John came along and started baptizing Jews. The high priests of the Jewish religion were astonished. What was he doing? He was bringing Jews back to faith and good conscience before God, not before men and their religion. In the Old Testament, when a king was visiting a foreign nation, forerunners were sent to announce his arrival. This is what John was doing. He was announcing that the Lord of salvation and the King of kings was coming to the world to redeem man to Himself. When John first sees Jesus, he states, "Look, the Lamb of God, who takes away the sin of the world!" (John 1:29).

Jesus did not just forgive sin or offer Himself as a covering of sin, as in the Old Testament. He actually took sin away. He made sure that nothing could stand between man and God except belief. This is still true for all mankind. The gift Jesus gave the world is bigger than anyone could have imagined. He took *sin itself* from the world.

Yes, the reason Jesus was baptized was to show His faith, but as the Holy Spirit descended on Jesus in the form of a dove, it became a symbol of the dove that returned to the ark. Jesus becomes the ark of salvation for the whole world. One man's faith, Noah, saved the world in his time. Years later, one man's faith, Jesus, saved mankind for eternity.

WATER

Water is frequently used to represent salvation; it carries significant spiritual and transformative implications. Throughout both the Old and New

Testaments, water imagery is employed to convey the work and presence of the Holy Spirit in various ways.

When the Jews are being led out of Egypt, they are stymied at the Red Sea. The Bible states that there were mountains to their left, mountains to their right, water in front of them, and Pharoah's army behind them. God miraculously parts these waters so the Jews can pass through. The theme of water can represent salvation. The Jews were able to pass through these waters for their salvation to escape being slaughtered by Pharoah's army. To this day, there is no consensus as to why it was named the *Red* Sea. Once again, the Holy Spirit is depicted as fire, and I like to think of the Red Sea as the sea of God's fire.

After the Israelites were liberated from slavery in Egypt, they were led through the wilderness—and they lacked water. They became thirsty and started to complain against Moses, questioning why they had been brought out of Egypt just to die of thirst in the wilderness. Feeling the weight of the people's complaints, Moses cried out to the Lord for guidance.

In response, the Lord instructed Moses to strike a specific rock at Horeb with his staff. Moses obeyed the command, and as he struck the rock, water miraculously gushed forth in abundance. The people and their livestock were able to drink and be satisfied. The rock that Moses struck became a powerful symbol of God's provision and salvation. This story serves as a reminder of God's faithfulness and the importance of trusting and obeying in the midst of challenging circumstances. Ultimately, it is an example of the abundant provision and saving power of God, even in the harshest of wilderness experiences.

Water is associated with cleansing and purification, representing the transformative work of the Holy Spirit in the lives of believers. Jesus tells Nicodemus, "Truly, truly, I say to you, unless one is born of water and the Spirit, he cannot enter the kingdom of God"(John 3:5 ESV). This verse illustrates the regenerative nature of the Holy Spirit, cleansing and purifying individuals, bringing about a new birth and spiritual transformation.

Water also represents refreshment and quenching a spiritual thirst. Just as water satisfies physical thirst, the Holy Spirit satisfies the spiritual thirst of believers. Jesus speaks to the Samaritan woman at the well saying, "Whoever drinks of the water that I will give him will never be thirsty again. The water that I will give him will become in him a spring of water welling up to eternal life" (John 4:14 ESV). The Holy Spirit provides spiritual refreshment, bringing fulfillment and sustenance to the soul.

As I mentioned earlier, water symbolizes baptism. And baptism symbolizes the believer's identification with Christ's death, burial, and resurrection. It signifies the believer's repentance and initiation into a new life in Christ through the work of the Holy Spirit. Peter said to the crowd at Pentecost, "Repent and be baptized, every one of you, in the name of Jesus Christ for the forgiveness of your sins. And you will receive the gift of the Holy Spirit" (Acts 2:38). Water baptism serves as an outward expression of the inward work of the Holy Spirit, signifying spiritual rebirth and the believer's union with Christ.

Water is a symbol of salvation. Salvation comes to the believer through faith in Christ and is sealed with the Holy Spirit. In the same way that God put Noah into the ark for his salvation, faith in Jesus puts us into the ark that God built. The ark of Noah had one entrance, and so it is with Jesus—the way, the truth, and the life. "No one comes to the Father except through me" (John 14:6). In Him, our salvation is sealed, just as God sealed the door of Noah's ark. Our spirit is sealed in heaven for eternity with Jesus.

Jesus repeats this with the woman at the well. As she was drawing water, Jesus asked for a drink. She asked why He would be speaking with a Samaritan woman, and Jesus answered, "If you knew the gift of God and who it is that asks you for a drink, you would have asked him and he would have given you living water" (John 4:10).

Water symbolizes salvation and the Holy Spirit in the Bible. It is associated with cleansing, purification, refreshment, new life, baptism, and fruitfulness. These symbolic representations highlight the transformative work of the Holy Spirit in believers' lives, emphasizing the spiritual renewal, satisfaction, and empowerment that come from His presence. The water imagery serves as a vivid and relatable illustration of the profound impact of the Holy Spirit in the lives of those who believe in Christ.

God made a covenant with Noah, promising never again to destroy the world with water. He took life from men by the water that was present at the start of creation. Water is used again as a new start for mankind. Peter tells us that this did not resolve the sin nature of man but rather kept man to the time of salvation in Christ. God covered the evil with water, but Noah was able to pass through this judgment because of his faith. Jesus defeated evil and took away the sin of the world, including death. John writes,

> This is the one who came by water and blood—Jesus Christ. He did not come by water only, but by water and blood. And it is

the Spirit who testifies, because the Spirit is
the truth. For there are three that testify: the
Spirit, the water and the blood; and the three
are in agreement. (1 John 5:6–8)

This passage deals with death and life. The water of
the flood brought death to the world, but it brought life
and salvation to Noah, his family, and mankind. The
blood of Jesus, referring to His death, paid the debt of
sin for mankind; it set us free from sin and death, once
again dealing with life and salvation. The Holy Spirit is
the life and truth, salvation of mankind through faith in
Jesus, and death without. The water, the blood, and the
Spirit agree; it is a matter of death and life!

Reflection Questions

1. What did you learn about the book of Genesis?
2. How can you apply what you learned about doubt, shame, and purity to your life?
3. What did you learn about the symbolism of water in the Bible?
4. How can that knowledge change how you relate to God or understand Scripture better?

10

DISCOVERING MORE

Then Jesus told his disciples, "If anyone would come after me, let him deny himself and take up his cross and follow me. For whoever would save his life will lose it, but whoever loses his life for my sake will find it. For what will it profit a man if he gains the whole world and forfeits his soul? Or what shall a man give in return for his soul? For the Son of Man is going to come with his angels in the glory of his Father, and then he will repay each person according to what he has done. Truly, I say to you, there are some standing here who will not taste death until they see the Son of Man coming in his kingdom."
— **Matthew 16:24–28 ESV**

*T*here seems to be much confusion as to what Matthew 16:28 means. To understand this verse, we must include the verses that precede it. As a whole, they become a statement of Christian doctrine that has confounded many. As previously stated, taking up your cross is to make a stand for Jesus as a follower. Whoever tries to save his life without Him (reincarnation, good works, martyrdom) will lose it. Whoever loses his life in belief of Christ will gain life eternal.

Jesus is going to return with His angels in all His glory. We see angels at the tomb of Christ after His death and when He returns in His glorified body. He will repay each person according to what they have done or practiced, and following Jesus as a disciple is how we practice our faith.

Now we come to the misunderstanding in verse 28: "There are *some standing here* who will not taste death until they see the Son of Man coming in his kingdom." The some who are standing here are those who believed in Christ before His death. The word *here* can be interpreted as "in this manner."[1] In other words, this can mean everyone who had ever had faith in God, from Noah to Abraham to any Jewish descendants who put their faith in God with the hope of eternal life. It is my belief none of these had yet died. I believe also that's why Jesus called death *sleeping*. I'm sure many faithful fell asleep, and would not taste death, while Jesus was still walking the earth.

When the Temple was being constructed, God insisted it be built according to His plan, a depiction of heaven. The Temple was built for the Hebrew nation to worship in the presence of God and was designed with an outer courtyard, an inner or holy court, and most importantly, the most holy place. It was in the most holy place the ark of the covenant, the mercy seat, and the presence of God were housed (see Hebrews 9). It is my belief that all who had physically died before the death of Christ could not die. They were kept alive, or sleeping, until Christ had fulfilled His mission. Remember how Jesus raised the dead girl in Luke 8:52 and Lazarus in John 11:11? In both cases, He said they were asleep.

This was also true of King David in Acts 13:36, who fell asleep and was laid with his fathers. Jesus did not say they were dead. They were asleep and still living. I believe all who were asleep before the time of Jesus were held in the holy place of heaven, not able to pass through to the innermost sanctuary, the holy of holies. They were being held in the holy place because Jesus had not yet died or entered His kingdom.

Jesus ushered to heaven all who believe in God by sacrificing His life and sprinkling His blood on the mercy seat in heaven (Hebrews 9). Most importantly, we read in Romans 6 that all who believe in Him are baptized into His death, burial, and resurrection. We live in Christ, like the ark of Noah, which was God's first act of salvation. Noah's family passed through the waters of God's judgment and were kept safe by living inside the ark. In the same way of salvation in Christ, we are safely kept for eternity in Jesus, through His Spirit. That is why we are called the bride of Christ—we live in Him. Those asleep before the time of Jesus could not yet die because we have to die "in Him" (Romans 6:5). All who are saved in their belief in Jesus die in Him, and He lives in us. This is the doctrine of salvation.

It must have been a glorious sight to behold for all those who passed before the time of Christ. To witness or see Jesus's entrance into the most holy place. When Jesus sprinkled His blood on the mercy seat, all those who came before Him asleep, died and were resurrected into Him. "Tombs broke open" and those who had died "were raised to life" (Matthew 27:52). They were finally able to die and live forever in heaven, in Jesus. Hallelujah!

THE COIN IN THE MOUTH OF THE FISH

> When they came to Capernaum, the collectors of the two-drachma tax went up to Peter and said, "Does your teacher not pay the tax?" He said, "Yes." And when he

> came into the house, Jesus spoke to him first,
> saying, "What do you think, Simon? From
> whom do kings of the earth take toll or tax?
> From their sons or from others?" And when
> he said, "From others," Jesus said to him,
> "Then the sons are free. However, not to
> give offense to them, go to the sea and cast
> a hook and take the first fish that comes up,
> and when you open its mouth you will find a
> shekel. Take that and give it to them for me
> and for yourself." (Matthew 17:24–27 ESV)

I cannot conclude my writing without commenting on this unusual miracle. I have read at least two dozen commentaries on this verse, and have yet to come across a good interpretation of this passage.

The tax trying to be collected from Peter was the temple tax. This was a tax to help maintain the temple and to pay for the daily animal sacrifices in the forgiveness of sin. More importantly, the tax can be referred to as a sin tax. Jesus was exempt from this tax, not only as a descendent of King David but also as the Son of God.

The temple was the house and dwelling of God, and Jesus, as the Son of God, was exempt from paying this tax. Peter knew this. When Peter was asked by the tax collectors, "Does your teacher not pay the tax?" his response was, "Yes." Because Peter denied that the Son of God was free, Jesus addressed him as Simon; however, Jesus spoke to him about how the debt would be paid by the one who had no obligation to pay this sin tax. In addition, Jesus did not want this to be a disagreement or misunderstanding with the sin tax collectors. They were not His followers at this time.

This is a miracle few can understand. Jesus agrees to pay the sin tax even though He does not have to. Jesus is foreshadowing the ultimate payment for all mankind, one He does not have to pay. On the journey for Jesus to pay the ultimate price for sin, He recruits followers to further the kingdom of God. Peter is the first follower of Jesus to understand who He is.

Jesus tells Peter to go to the sea, which represents the vastness of the world and all of mankind. He tells Peter to cast a hook and take the first fish that comes up. The love that Jesus has for people is the hook Jesus has cast into mankind, and Peter is the first fish to be caught.

When Peter opened the mouth of the fish, this represents the confession Peter made about Jesus being the Son of the living God. Jesus placed inside the fish something of value that will pay the sin tax—a true miracle. This is the value of His sacrifice that will pay for the sin of the world. In addition, the value He placed inside this first fish, His Spirit, is inside each believer who confesses Jesus with his mouth and believes in the Son of God. He paid a debt for us He did not owe, a debt we could not pay. Praise You, Jesus!

Reflection Questions

1. What was your understanding of Matthew 16:24–28. How has it changed?

2. What is your perception of heaven?

3. How has Jesus's sacrifice and payment of sin changed your life?

CONCLUSION

*T*he central message of the gospel is not one of condemnation or guilt but of God's unconditional love, grace, and the invitation to relationship through Jesus Christ. Our understanding of sin and guilt has too often overshadowed the beautiful truth that God desires us to come near to Him as we are, without fear of rejection or judgment. Jesus did not come to condemn but to save—to restore us to a right relationship with our Creator. Through His life, death, and resurrection, the burden of sin has already been paid, and the invitation is clear: believe in Him and receive the eternal life He offers.

The message of grace is about what God has done for us, not what we can do for Him. It's about faith, not performance. Sin and guilt, though real, are not what define our relationship with God. It is God's love, His mercy, and His desire to draw us close that define who we are in Christ. We do not come to God by confessing how unworthy we are but by accepting the truth of who He is—our Savior, who loves us without condition, regardless of our past or present struggles.

In a men's Bible study I attended, the leader asked, "What is the most difficult thing you have had to learn in your Christian walk?" With a dozen men in the room, each answer was about overcoming some sort of sin or shortcoming in their lives. My answer stunned the group. I said, "Learning how to rest in the Lord." The leader responded by saying it is difficult to learn and understand.

The matter of sin is over in my life. In that same Bible study, I shared that I do not confess or ask forgiveness for sin. That comment sparked rage in one member, which exposed how he was not free. I talk with God and still confess my shortcomings to Him, but not with any sense of condemnation. Rather, we share the burden together. Instead of asking for forgiveness, I praise Him that He loves me. God's greatest delight is having relationship with us. He wants to be included in all we say and do. Just a mere thought of Him is a prayer and acknowledgment He is with me. I live in Jesus, and He lives in me.

One of the greatest revelations the Lord gave me was through His name. I looked up the definition of the word *name* in the Greek, and it means "a word or phrase that constitutes the distinctive designation of a person or thing."[1] A person's name is theirs forever, whether they are dead or alive. When most of us end our prayers, we've been trained to say, "In Jesus's name we pray." I'm sure this tradition comes from the book of John when Jesus told the disciples He was leaving and that they could ask anything in His name (John 14:14). At that time, they did not know He would survive death. He left them with His name, which carries authority.

Jesus is alive and well, living in and through all believers. When I pray, I talk with Him directly and end my prayers with praise of Him: "In You, Jesus, I pray." I'm not sending out a message into the universe for Him to hear. I am communicating with Him directly. This practice has enhanced my relationship with Him for the better. It makes more sense to end a prayer by saying, "Because I am in You, Jesus, You hear me," or "Because of You, Jesus." Speak to Jesus. He is alive and well and is very real. He is a living, active God and not just a name.

I believe the greatest downfall of Christianity comes from not knowing how to fall in love with God. I often listen to Christian radio, and most of the sermons deal with sin and how we should change our behavior. Is cleaning us up so that we would act appropriately really what Christ came to do? He came to give us life in Him and to restore us to the Father.

I listened to a sermon a while ago about the love of God. When researching and preparing for the sermon, the pastor had asked his secretary to look up all the sermons he had preached on the topic of the love of God.

To his amazement, over his twenty-year career, he had only given two. This shows how easy it is to fall off the rails. Pastors don't preach about how to fall in love with God because few know how to.

I believe one of the most important things you can do to enhance your relationship with God is to journal prayers and praise. Our minds think so rapidly that it is often difficult to hear and discern our thoughts. The thought process will slow through journaling, which enables us to grasp what is most important between ourselves and God. Sharing your thoughts and prayers with a friend will also enrich your love of God, your love of others, and your love of yourself. Loving God, loving others, is loving yourself and creates a virtual triangle of love. Each side of the triangle serves to strengthen the other.

Christianity is not about how much you do or don't do—it is about relationship. When you desire God with your heart, soul, and mind, He will put His desires in you. It is that simple. Read the Bible with the intent to understand that God loves you. Study the Bible in a group to share your thoughts and burdens without condemnation. Talk with Jesus because He is real and listens. Love on others with Jesus "for where your treasure is, there your heart will be also" (Matthew 6:21 ESV).

The message of grace is about what God has done for us, not what we can do for Him. It's about faith, not performance. Sin and guilt, though real, are not what define our relationship with God. It is God's love, His mercy, and His desire to draw us close that define who we are in Christ. We do not come to God by confessing how unworthy we are but by accepting the truth of who He is—our Savior who loves us without condition, regardless of our past or present struggles.

As you continue on your journey of faith, I encourage you to embrace the truth that God's love is unshakable, His forgiveness is complete, and His desire is for you to know Him deeply and intimately. The gospel is not a call to hide from God out of shame, but a call to draw near to Him in trust and love, knowing that His arms are always open to receive you. Let go of the performance-driven faith that keeps you distant from His peace, and rest in the love of the Father who longs for nothing more than to have a relationship with you. This is the heart of the gospel, and it is the heart of the God who created you.

ENDNOTES

INTRODUCTION

1 Aaron Budjen, "The Personal Testimony of Aaron Budjen," Living God Ministries, 2025, https://www. livinggodministries.net/testimony.htm.

2 "1722. En," Bible Hub, 2025, https://biblehub.com/ greek/1722.htm.

3 "2316. Theos," Bible Hub, 2025, https://biblehub.com/ greek/2316.htm.

4 "4716. Stauros," BibleHub.com, 2025, https://biblehub. com/greek/4716.htm.

5 "G2476. Histēmi," Blue Letter Bible, 2025, https://www. blueletterbible.org/lexicon/g2476/kjv/tr/0-1/.

6 "Rapizō," Blue Letter Bible, 2025, https://www. blueletterbible.org/lexicon/g4474/kjv/tr/0-1/.

CHAPTER 1: MY STORY OF FAITH

1 Susan Pease Gadoua, "Can Your Marriage Survive When Your Child Dies Under Your Watch?" *Psychology Today*, June 22, 2017, https://www.psychologytoday.com/us/blog/ contemplating-divorce/201706/can-marriage-survive-when-your-child-dies-under-your-watch.

2 Richard Bach, *Illusions: The Reflections of a Reluctant Messiah* (Delacorte Press, 1977), 14.

3   Herbert Lockyer, Sr., *Illustrated Dictionary of the Bible* (Thomas Nelson, 1986).

CHAPTER 3: SIN AND HOW TO DEAL WITH IT

1   William R. Newell, *Romans: Verse-by-Verse: A Classic Evangelical Commentary* (Kregel Publications, 2003), 135.
2   "Advocate," Bible Study Tools, 2025, https:// www.biblestudytools.com/dictionary/ advocate/#:~:text=Easton%27s%20Bible%20Dictionary%20 %2D%20Advocate&text=(Gr.,%22Comforter%2C%22%20 q.v.).
3   Veronica Vaiti, "Understanding the Phenomena of Mass Murder Shootings and Social Isolation," Bhava Therapy Group, January 1, 2013, https://www.bhavatherapygroup. com/2013/01/understanding-phenomena-mass-murder-shootings-social-isolation/.
4   John Piper, "Greatest Book, Greatest Chapter, Greatest Joy," Desiring God, September 28, 2014, https://www.desiringgod. org/messages/greatest-book-greatest-chapter-greatest-joy.

CHAPTER 4: PERSUASION, HEARING, AND WORSHIP

1   "4102. Pistis," Bible Hub, 2025, https://biblehub.com/ greek/4102.htm.
2   "Obedient," Merriam-Webster, 2025, https://www.merriam-webster.com/dictionary/obedient#:~:text=%3A%20 submissive%20to%20the%20restraint%20or,whom%20 he%20feared%20A.%20N.%20Wilson.
3   "5218. Hupakoé," Bible Hub, 2025, https://biblehub.com/ greek/5218.htm.

4   East Coast Christian Center, "Worship = Worth-Ship," https://eccc.us/2022/01/04/worship-worthship/#:~:text=The%20word%20worship%20comes%20from,hold%20for%20something%20on%20display.

5   "4352. Proskuneó," BibleApps, 2025, https://bibleapps.com/greek/4352.htm.

6   "Strong's #3000: Lateruó," Bible Tools, 2025, https://www.bibletools.org/index.cfm/fuseaction/Lexicon.show/ID/G3000/latreuo.htm#:~:text=Strongs's%20%233000%3A%20latreuo%20%2D%20Greek%2FHebrew%20Definitions%20%2D%20Bible%20Tools&text=from%20latris%20(a%20hired%20menial,service%2C%20worship(%2Dper).

CHAPTER 6: REFLECTIONS OF LIGHT

1   Good News, "Constantine's Impact on Christianity," UCG, June 5, 2006, https://www.ucg.org/the-good-news/constantines-impact-on-christianity.

2   Acton-Creighton Correspondence, "Lord Acton Writes to Bishop Creighton," OLL Liberty Fund, 2025, https://oll.libertyfund.org/quote/lord-acton-writes-to-bishop-creighton-that-the-same-moral-standards-should-be-applied-to-all-men-political-and-religious-leaders-included-especially-since-power-tends-to-corrupt-and-absolute-power-corrupts-absolutely-1887.

3   "Grace," Merriam-Webster, 2025, https://www.merriam-webster.com/dictionary/grace#:~:text=%3A%20disposition%20to%20or%20an%20act,of%20kindness%2C%20courtesy%2C%20or%20clemency.

CHAPTER 9: GENESIS

1   This information was heard at a lecture by Dr. Hugh Ross based off of his 2008 book *Why the Universe Is the Way It Is*.

2   "Strong's G4566," Blue Letter Bible, 2025, https://www.blueletterbible.org/lexicon/g4566/kjv/tr/0-1/.

3   "127. Adamah," Bible Hub, 2025, https://biblehub.com/hebrew/127.htm.

4   "Strong's H120," Blue Letter Bible, 2025, https://www.blueletterbible.org/lexicon/h120/kjv/wlc/0-1/.

CHAPTER 10: DISCOVERING MORE

1   Strong's G5602," Blue Letter Bible, 2025, https://www.blueletterbible.org/lexicon/g4566/kjv/tr/0-1.

CONCLUSION

1   Merriam-Webster, "Name," Merriam-Webster, 2025, https://www.merriam-webster.com/dictionary/name.

www.ingramcontent.com/pod-product-compliance
Lightning Source LLC
Chambersburg PA
CBHW021149130626
46554CB00005B/1724